DEATH OF A BRONX COP

by

Tom Walker

iUniverse Star
New York Bloomington

iUniverse Star
an iUniverse, Inc. imprint

iUniverse books may be ordered through booksellers or by contacting:

iUniverse
1663 Liberty Drive
Bloomington, IN 47403
www.iuniverse.com
1-800-Authors (1-800-288-4677)

ISBN: 978-1-935278-37-5 (pbk)
ISBN: 978-1-935278-38-2 (ebk)

Library of Congress Control Number: 2009923039

Printed in the United States of America

This book is dedicated
to all my loved ones,
who live and struggle
on these pages.

In the days, months, and years to come, more New York City police will die.

The official cause of death will be listed as suicide, heart attack, even homicide. In truth, the death certificate should read "Organizational Murder—NYPD."

IT HAD SELDOM seemed a better time in that weather-cured, brown-shingled house, situated amid the rabbit- and snake-filled marshes of the northeast Bronx. Tonight, all thirteen rooms of the house rocked with raucous laughter and sonorous harmonica music as the Ryans held one of their boisterous, frantic, and not uncommon celebrations.

The winds that summer were soft and warm. The country had paused, groping for a new purpose after Korea. The following year, another less bloody challenge would arise in the Mideast. But that summer was a time of peace, a time to laugh, and a time to reflect.

Usually, these parties ended with everyone mad at some remark that someone else had made. Tonight, though, was different. There would be little time for acrimony or Irish melancholy. A family ritual was to be reenacted.

Earlier that day, Bill, second son of Hugh and Margaret Ryan, had been sworn in as a New York City patrolman. The entire family attended the traditionally brief, but haunting ceremonies at police headquarters. Five police officers were awarded the Medal of Honor—posthumously. Five police widows and their seventeen police children wept unashamedly—as did the Ryans—as did most there. Before summer's end, the Ryans would twice again weep together as a family.

After having administered the oath of office to the new recruits, the mayor had said, "One is thrilled to see the excellent young men we are getting into the department, which is the finest in the world."

Then, the police commissioner had shown the 122 recruits a certificate of appointment issued to Patrolman Matthew James Ryan in 1853. Ryan, he pointed out, had been wounded during the Civil War draft riots of 1863.

"The very spirit which prompted Ryan and those old-time policemen to undertake a difficult job is still present today," the commissioner declared, looking sorrowfully at the widows. The entire ceremony took thirty minutes. Its brevity, however, could not diminish the emotion or pride that the Ryans felt. They were the first fourth-generation family in the glorious and gory history of the New York City Police Department.

The party began as soon as the family reached home. It was still going strong as midnight approached. Rick, the oldest son, having refused his father's coaxing to join the force, shook his head, laughed, and said, "Another idiot in the house. Are you sure we don't have any German blood in us?"

Margaret, tall and slender with her long, black Galway hair made into a pompadour in front, cleared her throat and in a high, shrill voice, said, "We do, your uncle Sonny."

She was too late. Sonny had stopped playing his medley of Irish tunes and began to play "Edelweiss" on his harmonica. Margaret handed a drink to Rick and his wife, Julia.

"Well, I'll tell you this," Rick shouted, gulping his straight scotch, "I'll never touch that damn nightstick."

"Rick, not tonight," said Margaret softly.

"As far as I'm concerned," Rick continued, "the stick has a curse on it. Great-Grandpa got shot; Grandpa got run over ..."

"Rick," said Julia, "please." She shifted in her seat nervously.

"You must understand, Mother Ryan," said Julia. "It's difficult for highly successful people like Rick to hold on to the past—money has forced him forward."

"That's right," said Rick, raising his drink. "We prefer life and money over death—and that's what this whole evening is all about: death. My family loves death. You see glory in five dead cops."

Margaret turned away without responding. She was thinking. She started to laugh. And that's the kid whose bottom I wiped until he was thirteen, she remembered. Well, his pants are full of it now, for sure. She went back and kissed him on the top of his head.

Grandpa Ryan slowly extricated his slouching six-foot-five frame from the wicker rocker in one corner of the living room, looked at the pocket watch he wore on a chain, smiled, rubbed his tanned bald head, then announced, "It's midnight, kids."

Hearing this, Hugh Ryan shouted, "It's time, everyone."

The insults and retorts ceased. Tradition would reign for the rest of the night. The happy mob began jostling each other into the huge dining room. Servants would have loved the room, but the Ryans were working-class people themselves with no money or desire for servants. They enjoyed doing their own dirty work.

Margaret ushered each person to their unmarked but designated place at the table, according to the plan she had worked out.

Grandpa, Hugh, and Bill were seated first at the far end of the table. Next to Bill sat his girlfriend, Mary Faherty. The aunts and uncles came after that. Then the pregnant Beth and her husband, Danny, the first Italian in the family. Then the little ones: Kevin, Anne, and Janet. Margaret sat down last at the twenty-foot table, opposite her husband, near the swinging kitchen doors in case she forgot something.

That night, however, everything was ready and on the table. There was corned beef and cabbage, boiled potatoes, red wine (for "the Italian," as Grandpa called him), beer (both stout and Rheingold), and milk for the children. The pies, cakes, coffee urn, and brandy sat on a portable serving cart behind Margaret. And hanging from one arm of Grandpa's chair was the most important and symbolic item of the evening: the family nightstick.

Grandpa Ryan now rose, held his beer glass toward heaven, and said, "Thank you, Lord, for today. We pray that Bill will have a successful career and that Beth will have an easy delivery and a fair-skinned baby—a boy if you will."

Everyone shouted, "Amen!"

With twenty-five of the most voracious eaters and drinkers in the Bronx gathered at one table, the fair-skinned boy-girl debate, prompted by Grandpa's ad-lib request of the Lord, didn't quite equal the fervor with which the meal was devoured.

Then, as the coffee and brandy were being served, it was time for the ceremony to begin. Grandpa rose again, taking the nightstick from the chair arm and slipping the thong between the thumb and forefinger of his right hand. "This ceremony," he said, "is a reaffirmation of our family's commitment to the police department and the law. It has tied us, generation by generation, to something bigger than ourselves. It has given us a purpose, a job, and ensured our survival." He looked sternly at Rick. "Some of you might think that this is a weird and meaningless ceremony in today's high-speed world, but believe me, it's important to have an anchor from the past when things get rough. And sooner or later, they will … believe me."

Grandpa twirled the stick a few times to applause and then slapped it into his son's hand. Hugh Ryan, a graceful six-footer with thinning black hair, held the stick with both hands at either end across his waist.

Bill, a tall and lean youth, anxiously rubbed his left hand through his recruit crew cut.

"Bill," said Hugh, looking fondly at his son, "this nightstick has been in the family since the 1850s. Your great-grandfather, Matthew James, used it with honor during the Civil War riots of 1863 to defend a Negro boarding house against our own kind, Irish rioters, until little Patty O'Rourke shot him in the leg. Patty was sorry he did that."

He was interrupted by a few nervous giggles. Hugh continued, "Your grandpa here used the stick in the 1890s and early 1900s as a footman-bikeman on the Bowery. It served him well until his arm was broken by a runaway beer wagon, and he was forced to retire."

Grandpa interrupted. "I also used it to bang on the ends of bars when I wanted a beer."

"I've been using the same stick," said Hugh, "since I became a policeman. Now it's time to pass it along to you, Bill. Just one thing— never use it for revenge."

"But it has broken a few legs," Grandpa interjected.

"Pa," said Hugh in a pleading voice. "Remember, Bill, society's revenge is meted out by the courts."

"You mean they're supposed to do it?" said Grandpa with a wink.

Hugh twirled the baton and slammed it into Bill's open hand. The sound from the force of the blow sent a squeal the length of the table.

"It's done," said Grandpa. "Let's have a drink. Have you another Guinness, Margaret?"

"Right," Rick echoed. "I need another drink, too. I'm glad I don't have to watch this bullshit for another twenty years."

4

"Hey, Dad," said Bill thoughtfully, "in the past, the stick only changed hands on retirement. So keep it until you retire and then give it to me."

"You mean hold it in trust, so to speak?"

"Yeah, that's right."

"Okay, I'll go along with that," said Hugh, putting an arm around his son. "Case closed."

Uncle Sonny then broke into his favorite song, the "Beer Barrel Polka." Soon, everyone joined in the chorus: "Roll out the barrel. We'll have a barrel of fun ..."

Margaret hugged Hugh. "It's been a great day," she whispered.

Hugh kissed her on the cheek, as his right hand stroked her thigh. "It's the Lust again," he said.

Margaret smiled and nodded. Both then joined in on the last line of Sonny's song, "... for the gang's all here," as they edged toward the bedroom stairs.

THE BRONX WAS eroding rapidly, particularly the Thirty-ninth Precinct at the borough's southern tip. When the post-war migrations from the city began, the Bronx became a junction for those heading north to Westchester, northeast to Connecticut, and northwest into New Jersey. The well-to-do had already garrisoned themselves in Riverdale, along the Hudson, or moved up to Jerome Avenue and the Grand Concourse.

Whites, fleeing the inner city, leapfrogged the Bronx, but the poorer blacks and Puerto Ricans, crossing the same Harlem River, bogged down in the Bronx. It was only natural. In their zoot suits, they could only go as far as the three-nickel subway fare took them. To reach the suburbs, one needed seventy-five cents and a three-piece charcoal-grey suit.

As the path these new immigrants followed led into the Thirty-ninth Precinct, many Italians and Irish, who had sought the greenery of the Bronx after their own ghetto experience, moved again. Some, however, decided to hang tough and defend the neighborhood niches they had dug for themselves.

The Thirty-ninth Precinct quickly became a war zone with daily skirmishes between the competing groups. The poor newcomers, stuffed into rotting, roach-filled, rat-infested tenements, soon learned that the cruel, ruthless streets north of the river offered little more than their old world to the south. The seeds for the discontent of the sixties had fallen on fertile ground.

The commanding officer of the Thirty-ninth was Captain Marvin Adler. Though an excellent administrator, Adler's style and appearance irritated top police brass. Adler was different. He looked more like a Macy's floor manager—white carnation in his blue blazer collar with matching slacks—than a police captain. However, his non-uniform suit was always blue, a concession made to appease his division commander, Terence McGlick.

Adler, by his own admission, felt no need for personal, one-on-one involvement in the fierce and bloody conflicts pervading his precinct. He was an executive, and he intended to act like one.

Today had been another hard day in the Three-nine for Adler. He slumped at his desk. As he did more often than not lately when he had some time to reflect, he thought of his boss, Inspector McGlick. Why doesn't the stupid bastard listen to me? he thought. The solution isn't going head to head with these people—it's getting into their heads, finding out their needs, and reaching some kind of accommodation. Didn't the police commissioner assign me to the Three-nine because of my natural abilities as a negotiator? Why can't that big donkey understand that? he asked himself.

Adler pursed his lips in disgust and picked up his brown leather telephone book. He thought about his own needs and decided that what he really wanted now was a good hump. He thumbed through the brown book, found the desired number, and then studied it, silently debating his choice. Adler had become a big fan of the local ladies. He had gone native, as his men called it.

But before Adler could make his call, his clerical officer, a seedy-looking man named Tucci, suddenly appeared at the door.

"How did the interview with that dumped detective go, Captain?"

"You mean Al Hirschel, I guess," said Adler.

"Another shithead, huh, Cap?" said Tucci.

Adler winced; he always did at Sal Tucci's crude characterizations. "Sit, Sal," Adler ordered in mock anger, "and I'll fill you in." Tucci, designated as the Three-nine's corporate memory years earlier, took a chair in front of the captain's desk.

"Hirschel's been working midtown Manhattan," began Adler.

"A prostitute?" Tucci asked. His question, meant to elicit the particular sin for which Hirschel had been transferred, irritated Adler.

"Sal," Adler evenly replied, "I'm not playing twenty questions again today."

"Sorry, Cap," Tucci perfunctorily replied.

Adler continued, deciding to shoot from the hip. It was the only way with Tucci. "Hirschel was shaking down just about every man, woman, and child he came across. The guy wore asbestos gloves—nothing was too hot for him. He would take a deuce from a pregnant duck. He volunteered to work every Sunday so his Christian buddies could take their kids to church, so he could collect from every store that violated the Sabbath law selling beer. The guy was a vacuum cleaner. He never left the precinct—and that's the least of it. And you ask, 'How did it go?'"

"What was the clincher?" Tucci inquired, realizing that there was still something left unsaid.

Adler smiled. He admired Tucci's tenacity. "He was nabbed trying to shake down a high-class prostitute who was serving a city councilman on the cuff. That will do it every time. Free love is inviolate in this town."

"It's going to be tough to find a partner for this guy," said Tucci. "Any suggestions, Cap?"

"I've been thinking about it," said Adler. "I think it's best if you pair him with that black detective, Gordon Davis. He's a survivor."

"We're sure getting some winners lately," said Tucci, probing.

"We've become a punishment precinct," said Adler thoughtfully. "It's the last stop for most of them."

"Now, how's that supposed to make me feel," said Tucci wryly.

"You can get the hell out of here," said Adler, smiling. "That bull McGlick should be charging through that door any minute now."

"Well, in another six months, you should be deputy inspector and have a nice staff position at headquarters," Tucci offered as he inched toward the door.

"Good-bye, Sal," said Adler, cutting Tucci off before he asked another question.

After Tucci left, Adler thought about it. He wondered if he could last another six months in this asylum. Then he smiled, remembering the one thing that would help. He dialed Carmen Garcia's number.

TERENCE McGLICK epitomized downtown's concept of what a good leader should be. He spent much of his time on the streets, getting personally involved in every variety of radio call. No matter what the job, if McGlick was close by, he drove over. Downtown liked that. Innocent victims liked it too. McGlick was tough, both mentally and physically. He never improvised or questioned department policies, and it wasn't unusual for him to pull down a twenty-four-hour stint. Downtown liked that too.

Today, McGlick was driving himself back uptown from the Manhattan Athletic Club. As an Olympic light-heavyweight boxing champion, he had a lifetime pass to the club and used it once a week. Four other days a week, he worked out at Stillman's Gym in the Bronx.

Today's workout at the Athletic Club had been a particularly bruising one. McGlick felt good as he edged his green departmental Ford over the Willis Avenue Bridge from Harlem into the Bronx. Only last month, he had turned fifty-three. Yet, his physique was impressive, and he meant to keep it that way.

After checking in at the division office, where they weren't surprised at his earlier-than-scheduled appearance, he informed the division wheelman that he would be on the air and headed toward the Three-nine precinct.

Cops in the Three-nine had been responding sluggishly to their jobs lately, and McGlick decided that a little shaking and hollering, his specialty, was in order. If it was happening in another precinct, he would have probably called the commander and told him to correct the situation. But this was the Three-nine, Adler's precinct, and, McGlick assured himself, such courtesy was a waste of time. McGlick shook his head in disgust thinking about the man. It was more than a professional distaste; it was a personal hatred. McGlick despised Adler because he was a Jew.

Ironically, McGlick liked Jews. In the twenties and thirties, he had fought alongside them on lower eastside streets, drank with them in Tenderloin gin mills, and screwed them in westside bawdy houses. The Jews he knew were tough and dirty sons of bitches. He loved them. They were his kind of people. In 1927, Moshe the Jew from Brooklyn was the first man to ever floor McGlick in the ring. It was a left to the testicles. Moshe called it his Virgin Mary punch because you couldn't get an erection for a week afterwards. McGlick never forgot that week and all the overly seductive offers he had had to refuse.

McGlick had nearly married Sally Plotnick, a Bavarian Jew, in 1934. Only his mother's pleadings for his soul prevented it. A distraught Sally Plotnick sailed from his life that year to eventually meet death in the Warsaw Ghetto.

For many years, on quiet nights, McGlick cursed his stupidity and cried not-so-quiet tears. In time, the only salvaged emotion would be pride—pride in how the young girl faced death, a broomstick in hand, charging along with other young women, all flowers that would never bloom—an SS officer with a machine gun.

Adler, a Jew who wouldn't fight like McGlick's Jews, a man who refused to meet the precinct's enemies in the street with a club in hand, was, to McGlick, both a personal and professional traitor.

It was for these reasons that McGlick didn't hesitate to berate Adler both publicly and privately for his nonviolent stance. "Adler hides behind red tape" was how McGlick discreetly phrased it. An intensely private man, McGlick would never reveal the true depths of his case against Adler. Naturally, McGlick would never recommend Adler for promotion.

McGlick's reverie was interrupted by a call for help on 138th Street. McGlick decided to take a look.

Dutch Van Buren had been a cop in the Three-nine seven years now, always on foot patrol along 138th Street. He knew Inspector McGlick well, both by reputation and personal encounter.

Standing on the corner of 138th Street and Bruckner Boulevard, next to Call Box Thirteen, the tall, gawky cop was waiting the obligatory one minute after making his hourly fifteen ring in case the telephone switchboard sergeant had a job for him. Just then, the box rang. Cursing to himself, Dutch opened the box, picked up the phone, and said, "Patrolman Van Buren, Box Thirteen here."

"Yeah, Dutch, take a walk to 138th Street and Willis. I just got a call. A spic and a mick—ya like that, huh?—are going after one another with knives."

"Okay, boss," Van Buren replied. He hung up the phone, closed the box, and ambled toward his destination. A spic and a mick, he thought. Sergeant Klein was getting the hang of this place.

After almost a month in the precinct, Dutch had learned to walk slowly. It was not easy for one man to handle two slashing street people, who were probably stoned on cheap red. So Dutch continued slowly toward his destination. Maybe by the time he got there, it would be all over. If it wasn't, he would earn his salary. Hopefully, he would collect it—not his widow.

Van Buren proved lucky. A passing patrol car had seen the fight and arrested both men. One went to Lincoln Hospital; the other went to the station house. The crowd that had gathered for the event was still milling about debating the techniques and abilities of both combatants.

As Dutch was about to leave for a quieter block, he heard the approaching siren. He immediately recognized the green Ford and instinctively took two steps away. It was too late. McGlick had seen him and now came charging out of the Ford.

"Where are they?" he shouted.

"It's all over, Inspector; Sector John got them," Dutch quickly answered, hoping to calm the agitated McGlick.

"Well, what the hell are these people doing milling about? Break this crowd up!" McGlick yelled. "Get them the hell out of here, ya hear?"

"Okay, boss," Dutch calmly replied. "Okay, let's move it," he told the crowd. "You heard the man," he began to shout.

As the crowd slowly dissolved, McGlick turned and eyed Van Buren. Dutch could feel the steel-grey eyes measuring him, examining him, even daring him to meet them squarely. Dutch knew he was in for something, but he wasn't sure what form it would take.

The guy is just another shirker, thought McGlick. He always gets to the scene right after the battle is over. Probably a coward, too. I think I'll teach this guy a lesson. Look at that sloppy hat. No wonder we're getting our ass kicked in this precinct.

McGlick moved ever closer. Suddenly, he grabbed Van Buren's right sleeve with his left hand. With his right hand, McGlick ripped the hat off Van Buren's head and threw it on the ground. The crowd froze. They could not believe what was happening; Dutch could.

McGlick now let go of Van Buren and began jumping up and down on the officer's hat. Recovering from the initial shock, the crowd began laughing and shouting, "Stomp it! Stomp it!"

McGlick did his up-and-down pogo routine for twenty long seconds until his 225 pounds had completely flattened the object of his fury. He then turned and, without a word, got back into his car and drove away, leaving a long trail of exhaust.

Dutch was not confused, just angry and humiliated. A small Spanish boy, sensing Dutch's frustration, picked up the crushed cap, looked at Dutch as if to say, "This place makes me feel the same way too," and handed the officer the flattened hat. Dutch took it and walked off sheepishly, the derisive laughter and catcalls of the crowd following him and ringing in his ears.

Van Buren had just joined a rapidly increasing group of cops who had been victims of these seemingly unprovoked attacks. As his campaign continued, McGlick's sobriquet, "The Brim," would slowly evolve from a term of funny idiosyncrasy to a term with more hateful overtones.

FOR RAOUL'S TWISTED purposes, this was the best location from which to scout the street below. At night, from this roof on the corner of 138th Street and Willis Avenue, he could see any young female for three blocks. With an IRT subway stop and five Irish and Puerto Rican bars in that stretch, there was plenty of action.

For one moment, he remembered a time like this, after midnight in July. Raoul had stood naked at the yellow-chambray-curtained window of his apartment, looking while holding a black-covered book against his genitals. He had lifted the book, opening it to where the marker was to read a passage but stopped.

Five stories below, on the opposite side of 138th Street, a busty young woman, wearing green shorts and a red halter top, stood beneath a lamp post looking up at him.

Just then, a faint voice called from another room of the apartment, "Raoul, please, get away from the window."

He had looked at the girl below, then, in anguish, shrieked, "Thou shall not commit adultery! Thou shall not commit adultery!"

Turning quickly, he had rushed into the bedroom. He tossed the Bible onto a bureau and grabbed a half-filled Coke bottle before ripping the covers from his wife. She had lain there, naked to his gaze, watching him jerking the bottle feverishly while she pleaded, "Oh, no, not again."

That had been in July. On this August night, another woman would be the recipient of his cruel lusts. Before the sun rose again, his tally of raped and sexually mutilated girls would stand at six—three Irish, three Puerto Rican.

Two years before, in Puerto Rico, Raoul had received an award for being the best-dressed policeman in San Juan. That, however, was before the trouble.

A pregnant young woman accused Raoul of molesting her. After a police hearing, he was fired from the force. His dismissal was not due to mere fondling—that could be easily covered up. It was due to the fact that he had removed the woman's fetus with a garden spade. Although no criminal charges were brought against him—his mother's family was well established in political and ecclesiastic circles—Raoul was disgraced. Shortly thereafter, he fled in anger to New York with his wife and two children. Raoul had been impotent ever since—but only with his wife.

As he watched from his rooftop perch, a small, pretty Puerto Rican girl emerged from Rosie O'Grady's Bar & Grill—the Irish had abandoned it months earlier—and now stood on the opposite side of the street from where Raoul watched.

Raoul, having refused to join his wife and children on vacation in Puerto Rico, felt no remorse about what he had been doing since her departure. If he could not have sex with his wife, and since he considered prostitutes dirty, he took sex wherever the opportunity presented itself. Consent, Raoul had learned from his stepfather in Puerto Rico, was not the prerogative of women, little girls like his sisters, or, at the time, a little boy like him.

As he moved swiftly over rooftops, following his victim below, his body shivered violently and his groin tingled in anticipation.

The woman turned into a building on Alexander Avenue. Raoul, his sense of power growing, made sure that he had his knife and linen napkin before starting down the fire escape to observe in the darkness that sudden flash of light which would pinpoint his target's apartment.

Before the carnage was over, he would be in a rage, spewing forth obscenities as he humiliated and subjugated his victim to his will. After the act, he always left the linen napkin behind. Tonight would be no exception.

McGLICK GLARED with contempt at the 8 AM platoon, as the sergeant brought them to parade rest. McGlick held proof of their inefficiency in his hand: the monthly response-time report from the Communications Bureau. The Three-nine wasn't only the slowest in the Bronx to get to the crime scene; it was the slowest in the city. The inspector wasn't slow in letting them know how upset he was.

"You sons of bitches had better stop playing with your balls and do your fucking job!" he roared. "If your response time doesn't improve soon, it's red asshole time." The sergeant winced. What a way to start off a Sunday morning.

Finished saying his piece, McGlick walked briskly past the muster room desk, violently pushed open the swinging vestibule doors, and jumped the three steps to the pavement.

Two cops, lingering by the garage waiting for their reliefs, quickly ducked behind their cars to avoid McGlick's searching glances.

"He's on the prowl again," one cop whispered to the other.

"He's probably on his way to church," his partner laughingly replied.

The sun was still casting cool shadows over Alexander Avenue as McGlick headed toward 138th Street. The two cops sighed in relief when he disappeared around the corner.

✳   ✳   ✳

The Saint Luke's Ladies' Solidarity waited patiently as the speaker at this month's Communion breakfast searched his rumpled jacket and wrinkled pants for his notes. As he did so, a few giggles echoed through the hall.

McGlick looked up and smiled. "I must have left the notes in my old suit," he said.

The giggling increased. The old Irish ladies loved it. All men, they knew, were lost without a good woman to keep them organized. McGlick knew it too, but he was already married to his job. An occasional flirtation was the best he could offer.

Noting the mood of the audience, he said in a mock brogue, "Sure, I need a good woman. Are there any takers in the house?"

"It's too big a job for one woman," shouted a stout lady at the rear of the hall.

"That it is, that it is," McGlick agreed as the giggling turned to waves of laughter.

As it often did, McGlick's mood had abruptly changed. Like a politician, he could be tough as nails one minute then go out and kiss babies the next, some of his actions representing real feelings, other actions representing a mood assumed for effect.

McGlick now held up his hand for silence. The good ladies complied. "My talk today," he began, "is about the recent wave of rapes in your parish and on what steps must be taken to stop them."

McGlick's speech outlined his solution to all crime: strike hard and strike fast at the criminal. That had been the prevailing police philosophy when he joined the force in 1924, and over the years, it had become deeply rooted in his psyche. It had served him well.

As a rookie, he had been a promising boxer who quickly gravitated to the Midtown Manhattan Strong Arm Squad. This goon unit, a freewheeling and raucous bunch, included the legendary tough of toughs, Johnny Broderick.

Broderick was also a practical joker. Knowing McGlick's compulsion about personal honesty, Broderick leaked a rumor that Legs Diamond, the notorious gangster dandy, was gloating over getting McGlick on the pad. When word of this got back to McGlick, he stewed.

A week later, he cornered the killer in Shubert Alley. Diamond's denials went unheard by a raging McGlick, and Diamond was deposited, upside down, into a garbage can.

Even the police commissioner was not immune when McGlick's honesty was in dispute. McGlick, a sergeant at the time, stormed into the commissioner's office after a routine, pre-Christmas transfer caused some to believe that McGlick had done something dishonest to get it. Faced by a raging McGlick wanting to get his name cleared, the commissioner fled his office via a rear door.

After several days of such assaults, the PC finally, though reluctantly, issued a statement upholding McGlick's integrity. Something like that had never been done before and has never been done since.

By the time McGlick had finished talking to his audience, the hall was rocking with applause. The response of the crowd pleased the glib McGlick.

These Irish parishioners agreed wholeheartedly with his approach to the problem: strike fear into the enemy before he could strike fear into you.

It was while he had been in church, talking with and listening to the white-haired old ladies, that memories of his mother returned to haunt him, the mother who had been so different from the hard, filthy world in which he had to work and exist and the cruel, sometimes dishonest men among whom he had to walk. She had made a mistake with Sally Plotnick, but it was a mother's mistake—a mistake of love for a son. That, he could forgive.

When she died in 1949, he had stumbled badly and almost broke. The hard veneer, developed over decades, almost, but not quite, slipped away to reveal a softer, more sensitive and vulnerable McGlick. Through great effort and the unexpected help of Claire Reynolds, the senator's wife, McGlick pulled himself together to once again project the image of the cool professional.

McGlick managed a smile as he left the church. He was thinking about his regular Sunday evening visit with Claire at her Manhattan townhouse. The senator invariably left for Washington DC every Sunday afternoon. He hadn't missed a flight in five years.

✳ ✳ ✳

McGlick, surrounded by scatter pillows, lay nude on the living room rug. Claire threw him the senator's smoking jacket. "You don't like bare bears in your house," he said in jest.

"I do—very much," she said, grinning. "It's just that you'll look funny eating spaghetti that way." Her laugh was throaty. "You don't want to get Aunt Millie's all over you, do you?"

McGlick watched intently as she moved away from him to fetch her robe. He marveled at the strength in her trim, taut body. My God, he thought, the woman is five years my senior.

For Claire, McGlick revealed the other side of his character: McGlick, the Irish gentleman; the kind and considerate lover; the gentle-voiced friend who could listen for hours to the troubles of days gone by, making them disappear for at least a short time.

Looking into his kind, smiling grey eyes, Claire Reynolds could not imagine the other McGlick: the hard driver of men and himself; the steel-eyed, fire-breathing boss, who took no bribe, who let no man get in his way and made sure no man within his realm forgot it or sat down on the job, not once, not ever.

After the spaghetti dinner, Claire moved to the settee near the fireplace. "Shall we?" she asked invitingly.

"We shall," said McGlick. A rare, toothy smile crossed his rugged face as he realized how much he really loved this lady. She was a man's woman: direct yet sensitive, provocative yet ladylike, wild yet reserved, his yet not. They were the perfect match. She had the senator, and he had the police department. For now, they had each other.

HUGH RYAN slumped on the edge of his bed, a cigarette dangling from his chapped lips, as he coughed hoarsely. He got off the bed wearily, went into the bathroom, and spat violently into the commode.

Damn cigarettes, he thought.

Long ago, he had given up any hope of cutting back on the two packs he smoked daily. Reluctantly, he had chosen the cough over the forty pounds he added each time he stopped smoking.

Everything in life is a trade-off, he mused. Job boredom versus job security bothered Hugh that day. The insanity of his job no longer delighted him as it had for the past nineteen years.

Hugh had been a good cop during that time. He knew it, and so did everyone else. He wouldn't let them forget it.

A good cop didn't back down on those dirty South Bronx streets or allow anyone to operate uncontrolled inside his territory. Other cops allowed many things to slide—a bookie on one corner, a peddler on another—but not Hugh Ryan.

Bookies had to work from hallways unseen. Peddlers sold goods along the middle of the block—never on the corners where they could be more easily spotted. Prostitutes were either chased or arrested. No stickball was allowed on the main drags. Sidewalks had to be swept clean and kept snow-free during the winter. There were rules for everything, and Hugh Ryan saw that they were followed. Old-timers liked that. McGlick liked that.

Hugh Ryan missed that old routine. Being a sergeant wasn't as much fun as being a street cop. A street cop was responsible for himself and his post. As a sergeant, Hugh Ryan controlled fifty men, mostly from a new generation.

Hugh had his own theory about why things had changed after the war. It was that damn atomic bomb, he figured. Once those nuclear winds blew across this country in '46, it was never the same. With the fear of instant extinction was born the urgency for instant gratification. The new generation of cops was made of nothing more than babies trying to find a tit to suck on—and it wasn't their mothers'. On top of that, some became Las Vegas slot machine players—the big cash score was in. What was even more disturbing to Hugh was how some older cops had jumped on the bandwagon— and even some bosses. Self-sacrifice was a dying virtue—incremental advancement disdainful.

It was nearly time for him to retire, he realized. No longer would his view of the world be the dominant one in society. A police solution to the problems faced in the South Bronx was no longer possible. The world had changed. Technology, Hugh believed, had once again turned mankind's wagon train onto a new trail—a trail laden with buffalo shit. For Hugh, his family and their traditions would keep out the unpleasantness of that reality. Hugh felt his public career coming to a close. It was time to find a more personal peace pact with the world. In another year, he would have his pension and his freedom.

The smell of fresh coffee drifting up from the downstairs kitchen perked him up. Then, as he reached for his shorts, he frowned. He realized that he had to go to work today—his vacation was over.

For Hugh, the most depressing part of the job was getting used to the deteriorating, sordid Three-nine all over again. There, in those halls and rooms, out on those streets, was a world alien to and light years removed from the green northeast Bronx where his home, his family, and his real soul dwelt. Like an astronaut moving through another world, he played his role and did his job to the best of his ability. Maybe, he thought, it was because he was getting older, but it was getting harder and harder to gear up each day. He had heard how pilots, doctors, and soldiers had the same problem near the end of their careers. Cops are no different, he told himself.

For him, the only bright spot in the Three-nine was Adler. The man treated everyone like a human being. He would talk to you about precinct problems, ask your advice, and back you up if you made an honest mistake. The man had class—even if he was a bit of a fornicator. Hugh couldn't figure out why McGlick had it in for the captain. Like the rest of the sergeants, Hugh tried his best to avoid the inspector. Any meeting with that man is a no-win situation, he mused.

Hugh remembered the time he had responded to McGlick's mother's apartment. She had been ill and called her son for help. McGlick, working in Brooklyn at the time, called the Three-nine Precinct and directed that a sergeant respond to the apartment and take his mother to St. Francis Hospital. Hugh did just that, but the poor woman died before he got there. Hugh could never understand the man's response when Hugh offered his condolences at the hospital. McGlick didn't reply and just walked away. The man is more than a little strange, thought Hugh.

Hugh heard Margaret near the steps. She would come up and gently shake him unless he yelled down.

"I'm up!" he screamed hoarsely. "I'll be right down."

Hugh was thinking back to that night, over four years ago, and Mrs. McGlick. The other sergeant that night was Crenshaw, he remembered. Hugh tried to recall how he got the job. Yeah, that was it—Crenshaw's chauffeur asked me to go. Shit ... no wonder The Brim was ticked off. I should have realized it right away. Crenshaw sat on the job. He always did when he was ready to sleep. Man, it was a good thing his driver grabbed me. Imagine if we didn't try to save her. That would have meant real trouble, thought Hugh, sighing in delayed relief as he headed for the kitchen.

7

THE MONTHLY STAFF conference at the Bronx borough office on Ryer Avenue was nearly over. Usually, it was more like a lecture than a meeting. Chief Atmont, a small, thin man, had recited verbatim everything he had been told by the chief inspector at the monthly borough commanders' meeting at police headquarters earlier that day. Also present at this meeting were Atmont's assistant chief, Fritz Crown, the division inspectors, their aides, and several members of Atmont's staff who were needed to address the gathering in their respective specialties.

Nothing new was ever said at these conferences. Ironically, the list of topics remained the same every month. What did emerge, however, was a new listing of their priority.

It was the Madison Avenue theory of police administration: same product, new wrappings. In December and January, corruption was always priority number one. It remained on top for two months in a row in case one of the many bosses or cops who took their vacations in December got caught by somebody in January.

Most of those present weren't sure who that somebody would be, since each man was sure he was the only totally honest person in the room.

McGlick had said in jest at the January meeting that only he and the police commissioner were completely honest—and he wasn't so sure about the commissioner.

While it was not a side-splitter, the remark did capture the spirit of the times.

In February, the top priority went to cooping, a local practice of hiding in a store, bedroom (sometimes with a local female), or theater in a relaxed state of readiness.

In March, it was a tie—RMP car maintenance and drinking on duty (the seventeenth of March being St. Patrick's Day).

In April, it was personal appearance. It had come to the top early this year. (Rumor had it that it was because Xavier Cugat and Charro would be in the Easter parade and they expected a large turnout to see Charro's poodles.)

In May, the number-one priority was safety reflectorized belts. All cops were required to keep these strips rolled up in their handcuff cases, stuffed into the round opening of the cuffs, just in case they had to direct traffic at night, which all precinct cops refused to do because it was demeaning to direct traffic and anyway, traffic cops were supposed to do that.

In June, traffic tickets became the priority. The Bronx was not meeting its quota.

Lieutenant Gregory was called into the meeting to acquaint those assembled with some little-known violations that would infuriate the public but ensure that quotas were filled. He received a standing ovation.

In July, discipline became top priority. The complaint was that the sergeants weren't being tough enough with the men. Some of those present suggested that if all cops had crew cuts they would be easier to handle. It was the Nazi theory of police supervision: Degrade them, and they'll follow orders.

At the August meeting, superior officer evaluations had top priority as they were due in September.

This is what the whole ballgame was about, getting promoted. To most of the men at the meeting, this meant ego fulfillment and more money; to some, the main attraction was the power.

The three division commanders and Assistant Chief Crown all squirmed in their seats trying to figure out how they were going to be rated, although two of the four shouldn't have reacted that way; it was probably a reflex action from the past. This was the chief's ace card. He had made veiled disclosures over the past six months, when it suited his purposes, about their chance for promotion.

In general, it was safe to say, for one to get promoted in the New York City Police Department above the civil service rank of captain, one had to impress the borough commander—unless you had a political friend who could get to the mayor and he could tell the police commissioner to promote you, or you were friendly with one of the commissioner's top aides and he could get the commissioner to promote you.

If you were like McGlick, in both exception categories due to his Olympic status and his alliance with Chief Inspector Yates, it was only required that you support the priorities of those with whom you were allied downtown.

Ironically, McGlick's influence put pressure on Chief Atmont, who in turn would be rated by the chief inspector. Atmont would rate McGlick highly, though he felt otherwise. Atmont also had to take care in rating Crown, his young assistant chief, who had, in the past year, become a dutiful servant of McGlick, rather than the other way around.

After the conference, Chief Atmont asked McGlick to stay behind and discuss a growing problem in his division. It was a subject not raised at the conference and rarely discussed in a group; the subject was crime.

At best, the relationship between Atmont and McGlick was strained. McGlick knew he had Atmont by the cojones and was uncharacteristically obsequiously civil to him; he could afford to be. He wasn't being challenged. This deeply irritated Atmont. He knew that unless McGlick made a serious blunder, he was powerless against the man—unless, of course, Atmont wanted to put his entire career on the line. Until now, he had been the standard cover-your-ass chief. He couldn't think of any circumstances that would make him abandon a lifelong stance.

"That was a great conference," McGlick fawningly told Atmont then smiled.

"Right," Atmont replied, unable to disguise his contempt. Then he quickly shifted to a new subject. "You are aware of the rapist in the Three-nine, Inspector? He hit again last night. That makes six in three weeks. What are you going to do about it?"

"I've told Adler he'd better get that rapist, and fast," McGlick instantly replied. "I've told him to use all his resources and if he needs more men and equipment, to come to me."

"If he needs more?" asked Atmont, turning his back on McGlick to look out the window. "Don't you think we should get more men in there now?"

"I told you before," McGlick said, raising his voice ever so slightly, "I'm not satisfied with the way Adler is running the precinct. I'm thinking about requesting his reassignment to a staff position on the upcoming evaluation."

"Well, what's that got—" Atmont said, before being interrupted by McGlick.

McGlick answered, "I've told Adler, he has two weeks to nail this so-called linen rapist. It's his last chance. I've told him that."

"You know how I feel about Adler," Atmont said, turning from the window to face McGlick. "He's a good man. He has just had some bad luck lately."

"If he gets the rapist, Chief," McGlick answered with a grin, "I'd be willing to give him another six months to straighten out his command, but if he don't—"

"Okay, McGlick, you're excused," Chief Atmont abruptly said.

"Fine, Chief," McGlick replied. "Once again, great conference." He walked out smirking.

Atmont cursed. McGlick's arrogance was the final straw, he decided. As he picked up the phone to make the call, his hand trembled in rage. Atmont looked at his shaking hand for a few moments and then slammed the phone back onto the receiver. McGlick had him thoroughly checked, he realized. He had no one to call.

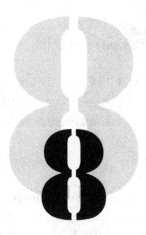

HUGH RYAN parked his blue Packard at an angle in front of the precinct, grabbed his freshly cleaned uniform and the family nightstick from the back seat, and with a twinge of regret and resignation, entered the station house.

As he entered the building, the cacophony of sounds coming from the working precinct hit him hard. The teletype was clacking out wanted and have-arrested alarms. The typewriter keys, like millions of sharp-edged metal teeth, ate away at cotton ribbons and sheets of clean paper. The radio blasted out rock and roll music from the 124 room. The desk sergeant was yelling continuously at two civilians. In one corner of the muster room, some cops were talking and joking. Hugh told himself to relax as he went upstairs to the sergeant's locker room.

Captain Adler, hurrying down the stairs, stopped to welcome Hugh back. "Be in my office in ten minutes. We got a heavy one," he said then was off down the stairs again.

As Hugh entered the small locker room, Sergeant Dan Crenshaw, already dressed, stuck his head into his locker. The smell of the room, as always, staggered Hugh Ryan. He threw his uniform over the back of a chair near the locker room table. Then he turned toward the already soused Crenshaw.

"For Christ's sake, Dan, did you have to pull this my first night back?" he asked.

Without answering, Crenshaw continued looking into his locker. Hugh knew that long before quitting time, Crenshaw would be sleeping it off.

While drinking was socially acceptable to Hugh Ryan, drunks were intolerable. The stereotype of the happy drunken Irishman annoyed him, not because it was partially true, but because most Irish drunks were really miserable. Dan was silent at first. His silence was followed by his being melancholy then belligerent and finally somnolent. Ryan dressed quickly and headed for Adler's office. Crenshaw followed at a respectful distance.

Captain Adler's office was on the first floor near the swinging precinct entrance door. It had been made larger by having one wall removed. It was furnished with a glass-topped desk, a wooden swivel chair, several armless chairs, a cot, and an American flag. On the walls were hung numerous plaques Adler had received from various colleges, professional seminars, and department courses. A highly intelligent, sensitive, and honest man, Adler was, professionally speaking, years ahead of most police executives. He told his men that he belonged to the human relations school of policing. The only hierarchy he believed in was Maslow's hierarchy of needs.

But pressure had been building against him. Evidence of that pressure was clearly apparent on his middle-aged face, and rumors were rife throughout the precinct that his removal was imminent. It was with some concern—for they appreciated their captain's ways—that the men had gathered in silence in his office while he checked out a pin map hung on the wall. As he returned to his chair, Adler sensed the supportive atmosphere filling the room. At the moment, it was just what he needed.

"We still have enough time, men," he told them, "twelve days' worth anyway. Have you come up with anything, Frank?" he asked a young detective near his desk.

"Well, boss," the detective sergeant briskly replied, "four of the victims claim that no one was following them. The other two weren't sure. What's interesting is that the four who claimed they were sure all live in this three-block-by-two-block rectangle."

He walked to the pin map of the precinct and traced out the rectangle. "We strongly believe that this guy is either cruising in a car or following his victims over the rooftops."

"He can't jump across streets if he's following them over roofs," one cop said, looking around the room for some support.

"That's true," the detective answered, avoiding any hint of condescension. "We haven't ruled out the cruising possibility yet," he went on to say. "We're checking out all personal and tag summonses issued on the night of the attacks, but it's possible that he simply goes to the street, crosses over, and goes up on the other side. We know that this guy is in tremendous condition. By the way, all six women stated that they turned on a rear light, a bedroom light, a kitchen light, or a bathroom light when they went in."

"Could he just be waiting in rear yards for a light to come on?" Hugh asked.

"We ruled that out for two reasons," the detective sergeant earnestly said. "Number one is that in two cases, he couldn't possibly have climbed up the fire escape ladder because the building didn't have one. Number two, we have had no reports from men or couples that a guy barged in on them, which would be the case if he was cued only by the lights going on. So, we are pretty sure he's following them."

"What's the rumor about some kind of napkin?" asked another officer.

"That's confidential. Right, Captain?" asked the detective. He knew by Adler's instant grimace that he had erred.

Street cops, Adler knew, hated it when detectives used the screen of confidentiality to withhold information from them. What the hell? cops felt. Weren't they all on the same team?

The cops in the room gave one another knowing glances then turned to hear how Adler planned to handle this one. Adler, for his part, realized that detectives had to withhold one or two key pieces of evidence in some cases in order to rule out phony suspects, as well as to confirm that they had reasonable grounds to arrest a suspect. But Adler also needed the enthusiasm and cooperation of the cops in the precinct. He wished the detective had handled this better, but it was too late now to recall his words.

There was only one thing to do. Adler told the detective, "I want them to have everything. The book is out the window on this one. Don't get too technical, though."

"Okay," the detective answered, still somewhat reticent. "You all have the flysheet and composite picture. These give you the MO, description, and a picture of doubtful value. The guy is always neat and clean. He uses a linen napkin to cover the victim's face and then uses the napkin to clean up with later."

"As to the time element," Adler interjected, "I've authorized two hours overtime for all of you, because the rapist hits between 10 PM and 1 AM, so I don't want to take any chances that we're caught short during the change of tours." He nodded for the detective to continue.

"We know his blood type from the semen on the linen," the detective reported. "It's type B, which is extremely helpful, since only 10 percent of the populace has B-type blood. Also, a pubic hair found on the linen confirms his national origin and puts his age close to thirty. We traced the linen to the manufacturer. The manufacturer gave us a list of his distributors. Only one, Marcus Industries, has any connections with the South Bronx, and they deal only with the church."

When the buzzing subsided, the detective continued. "We checked the local churches. None of the priests fits our man, if that's what you're thinking. But Father Hennessey, at St. Luke's on 138th Street, who runs a tight ship I'm told, says that some linen altar napkins have been disappearing lately."

"Needless to say," the captain added, "I've put detectives on a twenty-four-hour, seven-day-a-week stake-out inside the church ... That's about it, Captain," the detective said, indicating his spiel was over.

"Okay," Adler replied. Then he told the others, "Here's what I want done tonight. Ryan, you take ten uniformed men and cover the rectangle we discussed. Stick to checking suspicious cars and rooftops. Keep your RMP car and chauffeur, just in case." He looked askance at the wobbling Sergeant Crenshaw.

Then he said, "Sergeant Dolson, you'll be in civilian clothes with five detectives and five officers in civilian clothes. Stand by a moment. I have some extra instructions I want to give you."

Adler turned to Crenshaw. "Sergeant Crenshaw, you'll be in uniform and cover the entire precinct as supervisor of patrol. Inspector McGlick has been complaining about our slow RMP response, so keep the men on their toes. By the way, McGlick is on tonight."

❋   ❋   ❋

McGlick was pacing the floor of his Seventh Division office on the second floor of the Forty-second Precinct. Every so often, he did a squat thrust while waiting for his driver, Jerry, to return from the delicatessen.

Pacing back and forth, he kept thinking about the serious tactical error on his part. Several hours earlier, McGlick had received a call from the squad commander of the Three-nine detectives, a Lieutenant Harris. Harris had informed McGlick of the latest developments in the linen rapist case. Though angered by the news, McGlick congratulated Harris. He also urged Harris to keep him informed of the latest breaking developments. All old-time bosses had spies in key positions; information was power, the one thing they understood.

McGlick then chided himself for having given Adler two weeks grace. That had been a bad mistake. Adler, whom he despised, now had a chance to keep his job. McGlick wanted Adler out, and so did Chief Inspector Yates—desperately. And McGlick had promised Yates that he would do the job.

Already, Harris's detectives were staking out the church, and with Adler's luck, they would probably bag a suspect. That part didn't bother McGlick. He just didn't want it happening while Adler headed the Three-nine. Adler had to be removed before the rapist was caught. McGlick knew of two ways to accomplish it, but they went against his longstanding convictions on honesty and crime control. But McGlick had another big problem. He realized that the age cutoff for promotion from inspector to deputy chief was fifty-four years of age. In other words, he had a year to get promoted. If he didn't, he would be slowly forced out of the department. This might be his last opportunity to make it.

McGlick remembered what former police commissioner O'Brien had once told him: "Never compromise your convictions, but don't let your convictions compromise your survival." He would think about it. In the meanwhile, he would use his division aides to put some pressure on the men of the Three-nine. He decided to give his aides a little pep talk. Nothing like a little motivation. He chuckled. What can I tell them? he thought. I could say that downtown is planning a raid in a couple of weeks. Yeah, that will do it, he decided, picking up the phone.

❊   ❊   ❊

Hugh sat in the RMP car, slowly smoking a Pall Mall while his driver checked with the station house on the call box. Everything had been quiet for the first few hours. There had been numerous car stops and rooftop checks, but all were routine. Two uniformed officers emerged from a building and went over to Ryan's car.

"There's as many people on those roofs as there are on the street," one officer said. "You should see all the beer and pretzel parties going on up there."

"A hot summer's night, it figures," Hugh replied. He wrote the address of the building down on his DD5 (supplementary report) then said, "Okay. First check 975 across the street and then go eat."

❊   ❊   ❊

Raoul looked out the yellow-chambray-curtained window, not overly concerned by the police below, though intuitively knowing that it was him they were searching for. As an ex-policeman, he knew such procedures served as a deterrent, assuaged public fears, and, if luck was with them, captured their prey. Raoul, however, knew his real nemesis would be in the form of the plainclothes detectives, lurking everywhere, waiting for his first blunder.

Raoul realized now he had established a discernible pattern and method of operation that could eventually trap him. Tonight, he would continue that pattern, the thought of increased danger heightening his excitement, but tomorrow, he would consciously develop a counter strategy.

He went to his wife's bureau and removed a linen napkin. Only five were left. There was no doubt in his mind that he would use them all. The only problem Raoul foresaw was his wife's anger, upon her return in October, over the missing napkins, which had been given to the couple by his mother on their wedding day in Puerto Rico.

❊   ❊   ❊

The radio dispatcher called the sergeant on patrol to respond to a DOA on 141st Street. A voice suddenly yelled into the radio, "He's DOA himself, Central."

Carl Brandt, driving the snoozing Sergeant Crenshaw, winced at the remark even though it was true. Such things were just not said. Brandt had been driving sergeants for a long time and had seen more than a few drunks. Though Crenshaw embarrassed Brandt, he still covered for the sergeant. Here it is only 8 PM on a busy Friday night, with a radio backlog, thought Brandt, and the only sergeant designated for patrol duty is stoned.

Hugh heard the DOA remark as his men continued their search and realized he couldn't ignore the situation that now existed. He ordered his driver to head for the DOA in the hope of covering everyone. Before the night was over, he would do it eight more times, or once too often.

✻   ✻   ✻

McGlick's aides were gathered in a dimly lit third-floor division office.

"What could be so urgent?" wondered one of McGlick's aides.

"Somebody's in for trouble, that's for sure," said the division supervisor of patrol, better known as the shoofly.

"Let's hope it's not us," said Lieutenant Glasse, the division plainclothes supervisor. Glasse, on the just-published captains list, had only recently been assigned to the Bronx. The assignment of lieutenants awaiting promotion to this sensitive and corruption-prone position was the administration's way of trying to curtail corruption in the area of public morals enforcement. It would not succeed.

McGlick stormed into the office, shouting, "I've heard some serious complaints against those bastards in the Three-nine."

He adjusted his pants, tucking his shirt in, then went on, "I've received word that within two weeks—ya hear that? two weeks!—downtown is going to move on the precinct, and it's going to make me look bad. Ya hear that?" he yelled.

"I want all of you to spend your entire tours for the next two weeks in the Three-nine; you'll work the 7 PM to 3 AM tours. There are three of you, so work it out that two of you are working at any one time.

That's seven days a week. Work separately in your own cars." He moved toward Glasse's desk.

"I want complaints, at least one complaint from each of you, every tour. Hit the radio cars. Hit the footmen. Hit the detectives. Hit the sergeants and lieutenants. Hit the station house. Hit everyone hard. If they breathe, hit them. I want blood coming out of their rectums. Ya hear that?" he screamed, scattering the papers Glasse was working on.

The three were taken aback by McGlick's fury, especially Glasse, who hadn't witnessed a McGlick outburst until now. The other two could never quite get used to these happenings even though they suspected that it was all a big act.

"Are there any questions?" demanded McGlick, studying them carefully. He had them fooled, he was sure of that. Their weak "no's" to his question assured him of it. The stick had been broken his way.

McGlick now decided on a parting shot. "I'm going to be on 138th Street every night at midnight, starting tonight, and if I see a smiling cop, you're all finished. Understand that, Glasse?" he threateningly asked.

"Yes, sir," Glasse replied, totally shattered.

McGlick turned and briskly left, leaving them standing there with their insides churning.

Back in his office, McGlick congratulated himself on his performance. He liked the way he had singled out and intimidated the highly vulnerable Glasse. Great, just great, he thought.

It was midnight in the Three-nine Precinct, and there wasn't a smiling face on 138th Street; the torrential summer thunderstorm got credit for that and not McGlick. The heavy rains had chased the beer drinkers from the roofs. That pleased Raoul, as he slowly made his way across slippery tenement tops toward his special vantage point opposite Rosie O'Grady's.

Raoul knew how cops thought. Rain, snow, and extreme cold were their special friends. They would be relaxed, so he should have no problem with them tonight. He would have to find a new MO, but that was tomorrow.

As he left the division office and saw the rain, McGlick also relaxed somewhat. He arrived at a deserted 138th Street shortly after midnight. He liked what he saw and left to check on several disruptive social clubs at the other end of the precinct.

Ryan had had a hectic evening, alternating between the special operation, which dissolved with the late rain, and covering for Crenshaw, now safely asleep in the sergeant's locker room. Still shouldering Crenshaw's workload, Hugh closed up the temporary headquarters used during their search for a six-year-old boy. It had been the only successfully completed affair of the tour.

It was 12:25 AM when the police operator received a call from a frantic patron at Rosie O'Grady's Bar. The operator wrote down the information on a blue three-inch-by-five-inch card and slipped it upright into a special conveyor belt which traversed the distance from her station to the Seventh Division dispatcher.

It was just another Friday night homicide in the South Bronx. Nothing to get excited about, thought the dispatcher.

"Available Three-nine car, homicide at bar and grill, 138th Street," the dispatcher calmly said.

Sector John, close to the scene, picked up the job. Several cars offered backup for Sector John. Hugh, returning to the precinct with the temporary log, flag, and lantern, shook his head as he informed Central that he would be there in a few minutes. McGlick also heard the broadcast. Having nothing better to do, he decided to go take a look.

When he heard the sirens, Raoul froze. He ducked down and waited. An amateur would have run, exposing himself to immediate capture and subsequent identification by a curious onlooker. Raoul knew better.

The police cars arrived and stopped in the street below. Raoul cautiously looked to see how the police deployed. To his relief, they were heading for Rosie O'Grady's. Knowing this, Raoul slid comfortably down into his perch. He would wait until they left before resuming his hunt.

Sector John arrived first. Krauss and O'Brien, guns drawn, circumspectly but swiftly entered the bar. The bartender and another patron were restraining a black male by sitting on him.

Krauss saw the gun on the bar. He moved over then slipped the weapon into his rear pocket after making sure it wasn't cocked. At the same time, O'Brien cuffed the prisoner with the aid of the bartender. Krauss then went to see if the prone figure at the rear of the bar needed an ambulance. He didn't. He was dead.

Only after making sure the area was secure would the officers begin asking questions. A familiar scenario would soon emerge: two drunken friends, a violent dispute over money, one kills the other. It was routine.

Several patrol cars were already in front of the bar when Hugh's chauffeur maneuvered their car halfway onto the sidewalk.

Once inside, Hugh found the situation well under control. The deceased, he saw, lay face up in an Irish-rose pool of blood, his right hand clutching at his throat. The drunken killer, subdued and handcuffed, was sitting on a bar stool where O'Brien had put him.

Krauss was filling the sergeant in on the bartender's statement when suddenly, McGlick charged, like a wild boar, into the bar. Now the uncontrollable rage, the old-time cop side of Terence McGlick, emerged full blown. Everyone in the bar turned to stone as he headed for the prisoner.

Two wicked body blows jackknifed the gasping black man, a knee to the head catapulted him back over two stools to the floor, and a kick to the groin left him moaning weakly.

Krauss and O'Brien, on Hugh's signal, began dragging the prisoner out before McGlick could really get started, which would have prevented them from presenting to the court an intact defendant.

But McGlick's rage hadn't yet abated. Before Hugh realized what was happening, McGlick had grabbed the nightstick from under Hugh's left arm. McGlick now used it to mercilessly pummel the semi-conscious prisoner.

Ryan acted with swift and immediate outrage. He grabbed the nightstick with his right hand and began twisting it to break McGlick's grip.

The inspector yelled, "Let go of the goddam nightstick or I'll stick one up your ass!"

Hugh's anger blossomed. "Go to hell!" he shouted. "You're not beating this guy with my nightstick."

That would have been sufficient, but Hugh's subconscious foolishly fed him something which he had been wondering about for a long time.

"What the hell's wrong with you anyway? Is this how you get your rocks off?" he asked.

"Insubordination!" McGlick screamed. Hugh still refused to let go of the nightstick.

The prisoner was forgotten as McGlick turned the full fury of his wrath against Hugh Ryan. At the same time, Krauss and O'Brien, who wanted to get the hell out of there, began, once again, dragging the black man out the door.

McGlick and Ryan, like two bucks about to duel in a forested glade, faced one another, each with both hands on the nightstick. It soon turned into an even fight as each man tried to wrestle the nightstick away from the other.

Hugh quickly realized that McGlick, who was in better shape, would soon win unless outmaneuvered. Reducing his resistance to McGlick's thrusts, Hugh then made his move.

As the forward-charging McGlick pushed him toward the door, Hugh sidestepped without warning and twisted the nightstick sideways with everything he had left, throwing the inspector off balance.

Unfortunately, McGlick still held on to the nightstick. The two men slammed into the plate-glass front window, shattering it with the nightstick, and then both went flying through the opening into the street.

With that, the battle, for now, came to an end. Hugh had won the nightstick but was too exhausted to smile. The single word, *insubordination*, echoed in the night as a livid Terence McGlick returned to his car.

Everyone there, including Hugh Ryan, knew he had made a serious error. Each knew that authority is always right in the police department, even when that authority is immoral and abusive. Hugh knew he would pay a high price for his outrage.

CALENDARS ARE incongruous when seen from the reality of a cop's life. For them, time is measured in sets of tours; five four-to-twelves, fifty-six hours off, five eight-to-fours, another fifty-six hours off, five midnight-to-eights, then fifty-six more hours free from the grind. Round they go, set by set, shift by shift, off parts of days, working parts of days. The result is that one wakes up some morning, afternoon, or evening not even sure what day it is.

Hugh felt disoriented this morning. It had happened to him before, but never like this. Today, it was bad—really bad. Oh man, he thought, what the hell's wrong with me? I blew it. What a stupid bastard! One year to go, and I have to—. He kept shaking his head, unable to believe or fully answer the whys, ifs, and hows of the battle.

Had he overreacted? What would McGlick do? If McGlick did push through a charge of insubordination, did Hugh have a defense? If only he had watched what he said to McGlick. Question after question went unanswered. Hugh sat up in the bed. It didn't help. He headed for the kitchen. Maybe the coffee will help, he thought. It didn't.

✳ ✳ ✳

McGlick paced his office's creaky wood floor for more than an hour, considering his next move. In the heat of battle, he had threatened Ryan with charges of insubordination. Everyone heard him. Now, if he didn't back it up, the cops and detectives he had mentally and physically threatened for years, who had jumped through hoops for him, would think he was going soft. They would lose respect. Once that happened, he felt, they would no longer respond the way he wanted.

His division would cease getting the kind of results he was famous for. That in itself could threaten his chances for promotion and might even mean an early retirement.

For someone without a family, whose entire life was the department, it would be like having his genitals chopped off. This could not be permitted, he decided. He would bring charges against Ryan. McGlick's mind unsuccessfully tried to suppress the real reason he wanted a piece of Hugh Ryan—his dead mother. That bastard Ryan let my mother die, he told himself over and over. I had to phone the precinct twice that night. It took Ryan a half-hour to get to her apartment. It was disgraceful. She died because of one lazy son of a bitch. By God, he's going to get his this time, he swore to himself.

As he began to plan his attack, McGlick felt he was moving along in a current whose flow he might have trouble controlling. But he had to do something. Only he didn't do it immediately. He had good reason not to.

When McGlick didn't move right away, the division people were surprised. He knew the word would travel down the grapevine. As long as he was going to punish Ryan, he decided to do it with cunning. In all, he needed two days to straighten things out before he showed his hand. Meanwhile, Ryan would be lulled into a sense of false security. When Ryan did wake up and try to make his move, after charges were served, he would find his defense nonexistent.

The Ryan incident was the last part of the puzzle, McGlick realized. He knew it was the Devil's deal—his soul for power and revenge—but it was irresistible. From the start, McGlick had been a reluctant suitor in Yates's campaign against Adler for one big reason: his own personal honesty. Even the fact that he only had one year to reach chief hadn't been enough to persuade him to sign on with Yates. But now, with Ryan in the pot, he couldn't refuse. He tried to convince himself otherwise, but he couldn't. In exchange for helping with Adler, McGlick would get both personal survival and revenge for his mother. It was too good a package to refuse. He prayed that he wasn't making a mistake.

The first step in carrying out that decision must now be taken: The capture of the rapist must somehow be delayed until Adler was relieved of his command. McGlick now summoned a short, stocky cop, Silent Tony, into his office. Tony took a seat without saying a word.

The squat Italian cop had received that name because of his silence in front of a Brooklyn Grand Jury during the Gross corruption scandals. Silent Tony was Darwin's adaptable man; he survived by taking everything given to him as a reward and always keeping his mouth shut. It wasn't odd that cops had never heard of him. Few ever did. That was his strength.

With connections at all levels of society, both legal and illegal, Tony quickly gravitated to his present position after being transferred to the Bronx several years earlier. He had served many bosses in the division, giving each exactly what he wanted. Most were satisfied with his honest talents. Two used him as a bagman, and now, McGlick was using him as an intelligence agent and fixer on personal matters.

"I have two jobs for you," said McGlick. "Both have top priority. Do you understand?"

Silent Tony nodded without expression.

"I want the linen rapist found and neutralized until Adler is removed," ordered McGlick. "Can it be handled?"

"Yeah, it can be," said Tony, raising his eyebrows. "But it might be tough."

McGlick was about to reply, but Tony held up his hand.

"What's the second one?" he asked.

"An internal cover-up," said McGlick, handing Tony a list of people to see and actions to be taken. "Okay?" asked McGlick.

Tony looked at the paper then softly answered, "Okay, Ryan is no problem. Give me a few days on the other."

McGlick nodded, dismissed Tony, and then sat there thinking about what his next move would be.

✳   ✳   ✳

Captain Adler left word at his desk that as soon as Ryan arrived he should report to the captain's office. Ryan received the message and went to see Adler, figuring the captain would first commiserate with him then serve charges and specifications. He was surprised, though not entirely relieved, when nothing of the sort happened. Ryan asked Adler's opinion about the strange turn of events.

The captain was slow in answering.

"Well, to be honest, I can't figure it out, but from what I've heard, he doesn't have a strong case. And let's face it, that was a clean, even fight." He paused to catch Ryan's reaction to the word *even*. It evoked the expected tightening of facial muscles.

"What the hell?" Adler added. "He might just forget it."

Neither of them believed that. Both knew "even" fights weren't good enough for McGlick; he had to win.

Adler then changed the subject. "Did you hear," he asked in dismay, "that shortly after your fight, the rapist struck again, only a block away?"

"Do you want us to mount the same operation as last night?" Ryan asked, his mind elsewhere.

"Yes," Adler answered, aware Ryan had lost some of his enthusiasm for the job. He then added, "McGlick couldn't have picked a better time to stage that fracas, if his intent was to demoralize my men and undercut the entire operation." It was an off-the-cuff remark made for Ryan's benefit. Later that night, Adler would remember the comment and give it serious consideration.

Having said everything he had to, Ryan took his leave of Adler. Outside the captain's office, Detective Gibbs, from Homicide, stopped Hugh.

"What the hell happened last night, Sarge?"

"If you have an hour, I'll tell you," Ryan answered with a forced smile.

"Is it true both of you went through that window?" Gibbs asked in disbelief. "I saw glass all over the sidewalk this morning. It's amazing both of you didn't wind up in the hospital."

"We were lucky. My nightstick knocked the glass out before we went through. I'll remember you saw the broken glass when I go to trial," said Ryan, only half kidding.

"Hey, no problem, Sarge," said Gibbs. "I saw what I saw, and I'll say it anywhere." He meant it.

IF ONE WANTED to measure the honesty of a cop by how many bribes he took, McGlick would have been classified 100 percent honest. Man, of course, can be corrupted by many things; money just happens to be the most common. For some, corruption comes in the form of sex; for others, it is drink, and for a smaller, more select group, it is power. McGlick fit into the last category. He savored control over human beings the way a cat savors his trapped prey. His yearning for power proved unquenchable; it dominated his very being and extended far into the depths of his soul. In a job where honesty concerning money was regarded as a virtue, his obsession with raw, crude power was not seen as corrupt by his peers but viewed as strong moral indignation over the widespread corruption of the times.

But McGlick went deeper than that; beyond everything, he was an old-fashioned cop, the kind the department would soon deem expendable. But he hung on and kept climbing the ladder of promotion as the rungs below him were sawed away. A prisoner of his past, McGlick was forced to strike a compromise between his raw ambition, the corruption of others, his harsh temper, and a need for departmental allies. McGlick, like many in the police department, had become both a user and a tool of the system.

In his quest for power, he soon discovered what a useful device his honesty could be. Because it was necessary, at times, for pernicious chiefs and deputy commissioners to form mutually beneficial alliances with him, it was of much solace to them that all McGlick wanted from these arrangements was a recommendation for promotion, since that left all the money for them. It was a profitable experience for all concerned.

In line with those ambitions, the meeting that had been arranged for that morning with Chief Inspector Yates was an important one. McGlick felt the present meeting would push him even closer to the exalted rank of chief—and continual survival.

Jack Yates, a tall, red-faced man with an arthritic limp, welcomed McGlick into his Victorian office on Centre Street.

"Does anyone know anything about our business?" asked Yates, as the two men sat down.

"Absolutely not," said McGlick.

"Good. I want no one but us knowing what I'm planning for Adler."

Adler had not yet found out that he was on Yates's hit list. Yates liked that. He didn't want Adler, the police chief, or anyone besides McGlick and himself finding out about this.

McGlick was well aware of the interest certain city officials and mob figures had in Adler's retirement. Once Adler was out, Yates would collect a quarter of a million dollars. This was a very heavy contract. McGlick didn't know all the particulars, but "Red-Tape" Adler had screwed up while in Brooklyn. It had cost Yates a lot of dough and some sleepless nights. It had cost a mobster his only son.

McGlick quickly briefed Yates on his surrogate campaign against Adler and then mentioned the Ryan affair and the help he needed. With the chief inspector on his side, taking care of Ryan would be no trouble at all. Yates did not care one way or the other about Ryan, but if it made McGlick happy and he did a better job on Adler, then Yates was with him.

First though, Yates dealt with the matter most important to him. "You made a tactical error on the Adler thing," he warned McGlick, "but no matter. The fact that you gave him more time to catch this rapist can be remedied, can't it? I want Adler out this rating period."

"Well, Borough Commander Atmont—" McGlick began to say, but Yates interrupted.

"You do your part. Let me worry about Atmont. He'll bend as long as Adler don't get that slimy rapist. Now on this Ryan thing, what do you want done?"

"I want him brought up on charges. For my sake and the sake of discipline in the division, I have to teach the bastard a lesson he won't forget."

"Do you have enough to get him to trial without anything blowing up in your face?" Yates asked.

"I'm closing off his last openings today. I'll hit him with the charges tomorrow, and if you'll okay it, I'd like to begin transferring him around at the same time. That will really put on the pressure." With a distant gleam in his eyes, McGlick said, "I'll teach the son of a bitch to fight an inspector." McGlick had other moves planned but didn't feel it was necessary to fill Yates in on the nuts and bolts of his campaign.

"All right," Yates said. "I'll help. I'll call Atmont and push it. Any suggestions as to where we should send Ryan?"

"Staten Island," McGlick said with a smile.

Yates smiled back, his mind reflecting on the suggestion; then he said, "No, Staten Island, from what you told me about the case, would be a mistake."

McGlick quickly understood that they had to send Ryan to a friendly precinct, where Yates had pull. McGlick had a few ideas, but he didn't suggest any as it wasn't yet his right to presume on their relationship. The suggestions would have to come from Yates.

The chief inspector sat silently, figuring all the positive and negative aspects of the move he was contemplating. He would have to plan carefully. He couldn't very well allow the Ryan fiasco to blow up in McGlick's face before Adler was finished. "I'll call the orders section and have Ryan transferred to the Twenty-first Precinct. Both Cullen, the Manhattan North commander, and Stevens, CO of the Two-one, are on my team. There's no way Ryan will be able to get any complaints about you past them. Even if he does, he won't get past me," Yates said with a laugh. Then he added, "I'll give them a call and let them know Ryan is a troublemaker."

"Thanks, Chief, I appreciate this," McGlick answered.

With their discussion now over, McGlick took his leave of Yates and returned to the Bronx. Later that afternoon, Silent Tony called at McGlick's office and in one line reported, "It's all set on Ryan."

McGlick nodded, and Silent Tony left.

When he was gone, McGlick pressed a desk buzzer which brought the clerical lieutenant running. McGlick had spent part of the afternoon writing out his version of Ryan's insubordination. He handed it and a list of other necessary actions and notifications to the lieutenant.

"I don't want this generally known until tomorrow," McGlick said. "Do you understand what I mean?"

"Right, Chief," the lieutenant answered. "There won't be any leaks. You want it to hit him like a bombshell."

McGlick, never one to reveal his true motives, coldly stared the lieutenant out of the office.

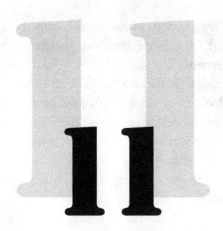

11

AFTER BRINGING in the milk bottles and enjoying the soft clang of glass upon glass, Hugh went down the driveway and across Dyre Avenue to the Nativity Church for 7 AM Mass.

It was a glorious morning. As well it should be, he thought. Today was the Feast of the Assumption, a holy day of obligation. Hugh, who had been pious as a youth, rationalized the nonattendance of his middle years as job related, but these last few years, he had happily attended.

The service that morning was nice and easy. Father O'Hara was up to his old standards and had everyone out in thirty-five minutes. Church was the last pleasant memory for Hugh that day.

The call came at noon. Hugh had been hoping it wouldn't come but knew that was unrealistic. Margaret answered the phone and called him over. Hugh knew it was the captain.

Adler's message was brief and shattering. If Hugh was convicted on the charges he had just been informed of, he would be fired. After nineteen years on the job, he would be out on the street with no pension, nothing—after nineteen years, nothing.

When Hugh walked away from the phone, nothing Margaret or anyone said could help him. Then the rage slowly appeared. McGlick's charges were a sham, Hugh thought, smashing his clenched fist on the sink. It was McGlick's damn stupidity that had triggered this entire horror.

During those first minutes, Hugh's emotions oscillated like a sine wave from rage to depression. Gradually, the cycles decayed and the reaction periods lengthened. Soon, he felt only cold icicles of anger. He needed that if he wanted the best possible outcome under the circumstances: survival.

He finally decided he had no choice but to fight McGlick. When he stared at the clock, he saw it was three in the afternoon. It had taken three hours to pull himself together—three hours before he was able to react properly; that was bad. A few years earlier, he would have been counterattacking immediately.

Hugh went over to the secretary, an old, inherited piece of furniture with three drawers and a fold-down desk with a glass-enclosed hutch on top for books and bric-a-brac. He sat down and prepared a list of things to be done. It wasn't much of a list: pick up charges, empty locker, call Two-one Precinct, call lawyer.

He called the department defense lawyer first. The answer he received was direct and simple. He needed evidence and witnesses to back up his case. A meeting was set up for the following week.

Next, he phoned the Two-one roll call to get his new squad number. They would tell him when his first tour was to begin.

As soon as Ryan identified himself, the roll man said, "You were transferred in at 8 AM this morning. What tour was that for you?"

"Today was supposed to be my last four-to-twelve."

"Let's see," the other man said, consulting the papers in front of him. "Captain Stevens wants you assigned to the Eighth Squad, which begins its first midnight tour tonight. So I guess if you come in tomorrow at midnight, we will be even with—" He stopped talking.

Hugh heard him mumbling to someone off the phone but could not make out the words. Finally, the roll man came back on the line.

His voice had changed, grown harder, colder, more distant. "They want you in at midnight," he announced with cold finality.

"Hey, wait a minute," Ryan said. "That only gives me a swing of twenty-four hours."

"That's what he wants," the roll-call man reported.

"Who's he?" Ryan asked.

"The captain," he answered.

"Let me talk to him," Ryan said, thinking there had been some misunderstanding.

Once again, the roll-call man talked to someone off the line. When he came back on the phone, he announced, "The captain said he don't want to talk to you. You've been told to come in at midnight tonight, and that's an order," he said, annoyed at being made the man in the middle.

"Okay, if that's what he wants," Ryan said, slamming the phone down.

Ryan was a bright man. He had graduated with honors in math from Stuyvesant High School in Manhattan, one of the best high schools in the country. It didn't take him long to realize the full extent of his problem. Until now, he had assumed his fight was only with McGlick; now he realized it would be an organizational one.

The power of the entire organization would be brought to bear against him. The more he struggled, the greater would be the pressure. He had seen it literally maim, crush, and often kill better men than him. Ryan remembered Patrolman Dober, who was targeted for an organizational kill because some reporter claimed he was drinking in the booth in front of the mayor's house while on duty. Already suffering, as many a cop does, from a belief that people really didn't like him, Dober was transferred from precinct to precinct. Within weeks, he fell apart emotionally and not too long after that, killed himself. Thinking about Dober upset Hugh.

Organizational kills, he knew, must be initiated or at least approved by a borough commander or someone higher up. It was the organization's ultimate weapon, one designed to ensure the organization's survival. As with so many other ultimate weapons, it wasn't fool-safe and often fell into the wrong hands.

Atmont hadn't approved this, Ryan thought; it must have come from headquarters. But why? That really didn't matter now. It had begun. That was the important thing. And he knew of no way to stop it.

Hugh thought about the many forms of pressure and abuse a man in his position could be put through. Time lost when transferred would be corrected months later or never. Days off—routinely granted for everyone—would be turned down due to the exigencies of his service. Normal courtesies extended by higher-ups became nonexistent in his case. Peers and subordinates, normally friendly, turned cool, fearing guilt by association. Stable relationships and established routines, which every human needs, become impossible because of constant transfers. Small details, normally overlooked, such as being late, become reasons for disciplinary action. Those were some of the things Ryan knew he would see and feel. But the truly Machiavellian maneuvers would take place unseen and unacknowledged.

Already, he could feel the isolation and hopelessness growing. He hoped and prayed that Margaret, Grandpa, and his family could relieve those feelings. So many had leaned on him over the years. Now it would be his turn to lean on them.

12

HARLEM, THE MECCA of black culture on the East Coast, was the gambling and drug capital of the New York Tartaglia crime family. In addition, it served the pecuniary interests of legions of dishonest politicians, businessmen, and police officials who were allegedly serving the area's huge population. With that background, it became a hustler's Disneyland, where fantastic schemes were devised and successfully executed, robbing the population of what little wealth they still possessed.

At the time, outsiders viewed Harlem as the Casbah East, an exotic place for late-night guided tours to exclusive nightclubs, fancy after-hours saloons, velvet decor gambling dens, and discriminating palaces of pleasure.

The other Harlem of hard-working thousands, deeply religious community traditions, talented artistic enclaves, a blossoming educational establishment, and an evolving business class received little publicity.

The Two-one Precinct was located in Harlem, just over the Third Avenue Bridge, not far from the Three-nine. As Hugh drove over the bridge into Harlem and headed for 125th Street, the hand on his watch indicated it was almost midnight.

The last time Hugh had been in Harlem was during the 1943 riot. He frowned in remembrance. It had been a damned nightstick which ignited the flames.

During the Second World War, Harlem had been the rest and relaxation center for all metropolitan military units, both black and white. The MPs and local precinct cops worked hand in hand at keeping the soldiers happy, steering them to respectable madams and gaming parlors. It was their contribution to the war effort.

One of the borderline joints had been the Hotel Braddock on West 126th Street; the local precinct commander found it necessary to keep a uniformed officer there twenty-four hours a day.

One hot, humid summer's night, Hugh couldn't remember whether it was late July or early August, the patrolman on duty arrested a female patron for disorderly conduct. For some unknown reason, an off-duty MP, enjoying the fruits of the city, objected to the officer's action. He grappled for possession of the officer's nightstick and won; a blow to the side of the head sent the bloodied officer reeling onto the soft, red-carpeted floor. However, one shot from the officer's .38-caliber Smith & Wesson ended the match. The MP, raising the nightstick to strike again, caught a slug in the right shoulder and fell to the carpet only slightly wounded. It should have ended there but didn't.

This spark began a conflagration which resulted in the lifting of the wartime dim-out, leaving Harlem, for awhile, the brightest spot in town. Had any enemy bombers passed overhead that week, Harlem would have been obliterated; it nearly was in any event.

Before Mayor LaGuardia, the police, and 1,500 black men and women, wearing civilian patrol armbands, could bring things under control, five civilians were dead and four hundred people, including forty cops, were wounded. Damage stood at five million dollars.

The full extent of the riot can only be comprehended when one knows that even rent collections were suspended for an entire week. Few landlords dared to tread where their armed collectors wouldn't.

Hugh had been one of five thousand cops and ten truckloads of MPs rushed in to restore order. It had been a tough week for New York. To Hugh, it had seemed as if Harlem had caught the full brunt of a hurricane. He hoped that never again would he have to experience that kind of terror. Damned nightsticks, he mused.

Driving along 125th Street and spotting a few new buildings and businesses, he thought the area had not dramatically changed since 1943. Then his mind shifted back to the present. The past was always there, but his own troubles had to be dealt with now.

Hugh was positive Captain Stevens would make sure he didn't learn much about the precinct. He did not expect to be there more than two weeks. It was part of the organizational pressure to detach a man from his regular precinct, keep him moving about so he could not rest, and thus keep him isolated and on edge. It was an effective tactic.

Ryan spent the night, as expected, on telephone switchboard duty, taking and forwarding crime complaints, answering questions, and recording rings and meal periods of officers in the field.

When it was over, he reflected that it had been a lonely but easy tour. He had been given the silent treatment, but that made no difference. He had been kept busy studying the charges, called pink sheets, which he picked up on his way in. He also planned for the long day ahead.

IT WAS 8:30 AM when Ryan, off-duty and in civilian clothes, parked his car on 137th Street in the Bronx and walked over to Rosie O'Grady's on 138th Street. The owner and daytime bartender, whom everyone called Fatso, welcomed him in as the first customer of the day. Ryan bought a whiskey then introduced himself. When he did so, the owner's mood quickly changed.

"Am I supposed to know you, mister?" Fatso asked.

Ryan didn't answer that but had a question of his own.

"What company fixed your front window?"

"Look, mister, I know nothing about a broken window."

"Who got to you?" Ryan asked, his anger audible but mixed with resignation.

"Nobody got to me," Fatso replied. "There hasn't been a broken window in this bar since I took over. I thought you'd been transferred," he added.

Ryan smiled grimly. "You don't know me, but you know I've been transferred."

"Hey, Ryan, you know the story. This last homicide will cost me one thousand dollars to the state liquor authority. Each fight costs me up to five hundred dollars. If I helped you, I'd have a fight here every night. And then I'd be out of business. You know him."

Now that he knew the score, Ryan couldn't really be mad at Fatso.

"Well, just tell me who fixed the window. It could save me a lot of legwork."

"I'll save you the legwork. A mob guy did the job. So forget it."

"Who paid for it?" Ryan asked, his voice rising, his interest piqued by Fatso's last remark.

"Forget it," Fatso yelled.

Ryan did not give up. "Was it McGlick who contacted you? Who was it?"

"Man, if you don't know, I'm not saying." Then Fatso added, "He's one of you."

With that, he walked away to the middle of the bar and began detaching his beer connections. Ryan knew he had found out all he was going to in this bar. He empathized with Fatso. It wasn't easy to run a bar and grill in this town.

Ryan gulped down his drink and yelled, "Thanks, Fatso!" Despite Fatso's wave, Ryan dropped a dollar on the bar and left.

He headed toward the Three-nine thinking about Fatso's "He's one of you" remark. Fatso wouldn't have said that about McGlick, Ryan decided. He rubbed at his eyes. He was getting tired. The last two days had been rough. Ryan knew he had a late start. He would have to work hard to make up for lost time, and if McGlick had erred anywhere, he had better find out about it fast.

The friendly "hello" from the lieutenant behind the desk in the Three-nine perked Ryan up. After a brief chat, he went to the 124 room and asked to see the unusual reports and UF 18 (city involved) file. He remembered earlier that day, that on the night of the incident, he had ordered a UF 18 prepared. It was routine. Anytime a cop damaged someone's property, a UF 18 form was filled out and sent to the corporation counsel in case a civil action was brought against the city.

The search for the UF 18 came up negative. Blocked again, Ryan thought. "What tour is this for you, Pete?" he asked the cop in the 124 room, trying to sound as if he were just making conversation.

"My last one, thank God."

"By the way, Pete, has anyone from division been looking at the 18 file in the last few days?"

Pete squinted as he thought that one over. "No, I don't remember seeing anyone. The only division guy around in the last couple days was Silent Tony, and he was checking property vouchers on a gambling arrest."

"Thanks anyway," Ryan said. He had never heard of Silent Tony and wondered about the nickname. "By the way, how come they call him Silent Tony?"

"I don't know. I heard one of the plainclothesmen call him that behind his back. Maybe he's just a quiet guy—"

"Yeah, probably," Ryan answered while thumbing through the unusual reports (UF 49s). There it was, "homicide in bar and grill," right where it was supposed to be. Unfortunately, nothing in the report could help him. There was no mention of a broken window, and under the caption "Forms prepared," there was no mention that a UF 18 had been made out.

Then it hit Ryan. This report was an original. Originals were never kept for precinct file purposes; they went directly to the chief inspector's office. Obviously, this was a forgery. This was going to be a tough one, Hugh realized, if he had to do all the digging himself. He was beginning to get depressed. This kept getting deeper and deeper, and already, he was exhausted.

Captain Adler, returning from a staff meeting, observed Ryan writing on a pad near the muster room desk. Adler had been thinking for some time about an offer he planned to make. Ryan's exhausted look prompted him to delay no longer. When Ryan looked up and noticed Adler, the captain motioned his former subordinate into his office.

Once Ryan was inside, Adler asked, "What's up, Hugh?"

"I'm trying to get witnesses and evidence," explained the weary Ryan. "Krauss and O'Brien are off. I'll call them at home. I'm waiting for Gibbs from Homicide."

Without hesitation, Adler looked Hugh in the eye and said, "I'll be a character witness at your trial."

The statement came so suddenly, Ryan wasn't sure he'd heard right.

"I'm sorry. I don't think ..."

He did not get a chance to finish as Adler again said, "I'll be your character witness, if you want me to."

Ryan could feel the emotion rising in his heavy chest and then jump to his quivering cheeks. Adler, sensing Ryan's reaction and embarrassment, patted him on the arm and said, "I'll be right back."

Ryan hadn't realized how vulnerable he had become. Now he knew. The offer made by Adler, at much personal risk, was greatly appreciated and would be accepted. However, Ryan feared that in his present emotional state, he wasn't in top condition for the long fight ahead.

Adler peeked into his office. Seeing that Ryan had sufficiently recovered, he entered. Ryan smiled and grabbed Adler's hand.

"Thanks, Cap," Hugh said. "I realize the chance you're taking. McGlick isn't exactly one of your pals."

Adler patted Hugh on the back and stepped back. "It isn't masochism, Hugh," said Adler with sincerity. "You've been my best sergeant; you deserve my support."

Hugh continued to shake Adler's hand.

"Thanks, Captain," he said. "I really appreciate it—believe me."

Hugh went to find Detective Gibbs.

Ryan was surprised for the second time that day when Gibbs reaffirmed his previous commitment to testify that he had observed a broken window when visiting the location of the homicide on the night of the fight. After thanking Gibbs, Ryan went home for some sleep. He had to be back at the Two-one at midnight.

Ryan felt good driving home, not because he thought he could win, but because at least two men had shown the decency and courage to stand up and be counted. Ryan appreciated the difficulty of such an act. A man stands up, not just to help others, but because of some inner force which tells him that for his own self-respect he must do it.

After Hugh went to bed, Margaret, Grandpa, and Bill sat at the kitchen table talking while the kids watched *The Goldbergs* on TV.

"He doesn't look good," Margaret said with concern.

"I've told one of my instructors about this," Bill said, "and he didn't believe me." That annoyed Bill.

"Look what I found," Grandpa said, putting a notebook on the table and opening it to the first page. It read:

1. Stay away from division!
2. Borough office, chief inspector's office—check unusual report and see if UF 18 prepared.
3. Bar—N.G., mob replaced window?
4. D.A.—Talk to prisoner? Too risky.
5. Call X O'Brien (914-555-6103) and X Krauss (374-6974)
V   Adler—character
V   Gibbs—saw window   <u>NEED HELP</u>

"Margaret, Bill, do you see what I mean?" Grandpa said, pointing to the underlined words, *need help.*

"Oh boy," Bill exclaimed. Margaret's hands trembled.

"When he wakes up," Grandpa announced, "I'm going to tell him that we'll try to help." Each of them nodded, though not exactly sure just how they might do it. They knew what this ordeal was costing Hugh.

Grandpa then copied the pad's contents onto a sheet of paper and replaced the pad where he found it, next to the phone.

Earlier, when Hugh arrived home, he had eaten lightly then made two phone calls before going to bed. Once in bed, however, he had lain awake, thinking about the refusal of O'Brien and Krauss to get involved. They claimed they had removed the prisoner from the bar, leaving McGlick and Ryan still talking inside. After putting their prisoner into the patrol car, they left. "No, no, no" were the answers to his questions about the nightstick, the fight, and the window.

Sitting in his chair, looking down at his copied sheet, Grandpa realized what the Xs and Vs meant: Two had offered help; two had refused.

IT WAS MIDNIGHT. Detective Second Grade Gordon Davis, a tall, lean, wheat-germ-eating black man, sat reading a novel in the choir loft of Saint Luke's Church, glancing up frequently to observe the young woman in the front pew. Suddenly, he heard the church door open and shut, but no one appeared below. That was the second time in the last five minutes that this had happened.

Davis put down his book, a turn-of-the-century police novel titled *Behind the Green Lights,* and called his outside partner, Al Hirschel, on the portable radio he had with him.

"Is anyone near the door of the church?"

"It's pretty damn dark up there," Hirschel answered, looking out of the unmarked police car he sat in, "but I think I see a figure sitting on the steps. Why?"

"Just keep an eye on him."

The young woman had now risen, blessed herself, and walked out. Hirschel watched her come down the church steps and move along 138th Street toward St. Ann's Avenue.

The figure on the steps, a man, had now risen and seemed to be following her. Hirschel alerted Davis over the radio; they had a quick conversation debating what course they should follow.

Hirschel wanted to stay with the stakeout. Davis had a feeling something bad was about to happen. They compromised. Instead of following the man, they would stop and question him.

Davis left his position and went outside to where Hirschel and his car were waiting. They sped off then stopped just as quickly twenty-five feet ahead of the walking man, who froze as the two detectives emerged from the car and approached him.

Unshaven and shabbily dressed, the suspect said in a drunken voice, "Man, I do nothing."

Hirschel, a short and obese but handsome man, smiled, shook his head, and told Davis, "This ain't the guy, Gordon."

A quick pat down by Davis produced a switchblade, which was not unusual for that area.

"Let's see some ID," Davis told the man. The drunk fumbled around in his pockets for several seconds but came up empty.

"I have nothing," he told them.

Hirschel's expression told Davis to forget about the knife; his glance said that Hirschel wanted to get back to the stakeout.

Davis ignored his partner and went on asking questions. "What's your name?" he asked while going through the man's pockets, finding only a single key.

"Hector Cruz."

"Where do you live?" Davis roughly asked.

"The project on Alexander Avenue."

"Let's take him home," Davis said. He had no intention of doing so but wanted to test the man's reaction.

"Thank you," Cruz replied.

Hirschel was getting annoyed at his partner's persistence and delay and wasn't shy in saying so. "He ain't the fuckin' guy, Gordon. It ain't the MO or the description."

Davis put the switchblade into his pocket and returned to the car.

"Blow, pal," Hirschel told the man.

"What about the lift?"

"Another time, amigo," Hirschel answered, moving swiftly toward the car.

Raoul smiled as the two detectives drove away. It had been a close call but he had handled it well, he thought. The change of image, the altered MO had worked.

✳ ✳ ✳

Raoul ran a hand across his lower abdomen where the linen napkin was smoothly hidden by the band of his jockey shorts. It was now 12:30

AM. For safety's sake, he decided to abandon his quest for that night. What bothered him was that he hadn't spotted those detectives earlier. Where did they come from?

The phone at the Two-one rang. Ryan picked it up. "Two-one sergeant," he said. The man on the other end identified himself. "Okay, you're in," Ryan answered. He found Officer Jackson's name on the TS sheet and under the 2 AM column wrote in the time of the ring, 15.

His mind then wandered to other matters. The family concern, displayed earlier that day, had touched Hugh deeply. Margaret wanted him to call in sick. Grandpa offered to follow up some leads starting in the morning, and Bill offered his nights and weekends.

Hugh said "no" to Margaret's request and "yes" to the other offers. It was important to them, so it was important to him. Had the rest of the family known about his dilemma they also would have offered their help. But he told Margaret, Grandpa, and Bill that it was best if their group remained small.

A scream punctured his thoughts. The scream turned into many screams that grew louder as they reached the station house. Ryan grabbed his nightstick, hanging from a nail next to his chair, and rose. The lieutenant next to him did likewise.

A screaming man, terror etched across his face and clearly evident in his voice, pushed open the vestibule door to the muster room with his left hand and rushed inside. Hugh quickly saw that the man's right hand was gone and that the remaining stump was bleeding profusely. Within seconds, the cause of the terror, a screaming black man carrying a raised machete, rushed through the vestibule door.

The bleeding man raced past the desk into the sitting room. As he did so, the lieutenant moved out to block the pursuer, a drawn, cocked .38 in his right hand, and a nightstick in his left. At the same time, Ryan moved in from the rear.

The lieutenant screamed, "Drop it or you're a dead motherfucker," his language purposely foul so the running man would know he meant business.

The pursuer stopped for one second only because he sensed someone closing in from the rear. He turned and swung the machete wildly. Ryan's raised nightstick stopped the dull blade, but the force of the blow knocked him to the floor. The attacker moved in to finish the job. As he did so, the lieutenant laid the full power of his nightstick across the back of the man's neck, sending him reeling unconscious to the floor. For Ryan, salvation had come none too soon.

Several cops emerged from elsewhere in the precinct to handcuff the comatose swordsman, while the lieutenant went to help the maimed victim.

The attack, it later turned out, was the result of a fight over a woman. The incident left Ryan breathing heavily. He began to perspire and felt a dull pain in his left shoulder. Finally, he flopped down into a chair. Sitting there, he was sure the capsules his chiropractor had given him for his bursitis would clear things up. The pain rapidly passed, and he soon forgot about it.

Before going home, Gordon Davis threw the switchblade he had confiscated into a box at the bottom of his locker. There, the knife rested among others he had taken from various nuts on the streets of the Three-nine Precinct. The box was nearly full.

Reports had been pouring into McGlick's office all morning. Captain Stevens called to give a status report on Ryan; a captain from the police academy phoned to report something he had heard from an instructor; a sergeant called to catalogue Ryan's activities regarding certain reports; and a chief phoned to inform McGlick about Adler's commitment to Ryan. The last message caused McGlick to repeatedly pound his desk in rage.

The phone was often used for such intelligence gathering, but if the information had broader significance, it was reported in person. For that reason, McGlick again called Silent Tony to his office.

When Tony arrived, McGlick motioned him to a chair in the corner. Tony sat down and quickly delivered his message in a carefully worded, staccato burst.

"On the tap, two calls, both cops, he was turned down."

McGlick nodded. Having Ryan's phone tapped was another maneuver he used to ensure that the best intelligence flowed into his office. This was a very delicate operation, and he wanted no mistakes made—not one.

"Keep the tap on his phone a while longer," McGlick said, lowering his voice to match Tony's. "I'll tell you when to remove it."

Tony then went on. "Ryan was at the bar and got nothing."

"Yeah," said McGlick, "it was reported to me that he checked the unusuals and UF 18 file at the Three-nine. What about those?"

"No problems," said Tony. "Unusuals are okay, even the CI's copy was removed." He took a sheet of paper from his pocket. "I just got this from the corporation counsel."

"Good," McGlick said as he reached for the copy of the UF 18.

"One problem," Tony said. "Gibbs, homicide detective, won't cave in. Needs your touch."

"What?" said McGlick, shocked. Tony, hearing someone outside the door, put an index finger up to his lips. McGlick was furious but said nothing more.

The inspector quickly reflected back on what Ryan had been doing and realized the sergeant had more spunk than expected. McGlick's face reddened. He realized that if Ryan probed too hard, higher-ups might notice, and questions could get asked. Somehow, this had to be stopped.

Turning his mind to Adler, McGlick reflected that the captain's siding with Ryan did not really mean that much. Ryan needed hard evidence more than character witnesses. And he didn't have it. However, the fact that Adler had moved against McGlick would, in the end, prove to be an asset. It made McGlick's task of getting rid of the troublesome captain that much easier.

But there was still Gibbs. He could create the element of doubt Ryan needed to beat the insubordination charges at the departmental trial. An immediate stop had to be put to that.

McGlick rose from his chair, his face pale, his eyes burning with final-round intensity, and, without a word, he strode from the room, leaving Tony in his corner.

✳   ✳   ✳

Margaret had seen how tired Hugh was when he got home. After telling her about the machete attack and how the nightstick and the lieutenant helped save him, Hugh went to bed.

At 10:00 PM, Margaret went upstairs to wake her husband for the midnight tour but found him sound asleep. Being a good wife, she decided to call him in sick instead of waking him. Margaret knew Hugh would be annoyed, but she did what she had to. Grandpa agreed. Hugh finally woke at 1:00 PM the following day, twenty-six hours after he had gone to bed, and he was less annoyed than expected.

15

GRANDPA, AKA John Brendan Ryan, or just J.B. to his cronies, had been appointed to the police force in 1896 by none other than Teddy Roosevelt. That was two years before the towns, cities, and villages were consolidated into a single entity, New York City. For those who served under Roosevelt, no police commissioner since had measured up to "Teddy Bear," as his men affectionately called him. Grandpa felt that in addition to providing charismatic leadership and strong support for his men, Roosevelt, and this was often overlooked, was a great innovator. He upgraded recruitment standards, based appointments on merit not politics, standardized equipment, hired the first female secretary to work for the department, pushed training needs, and hired such minorities as the Irish and Jews. Roosevelt's admiration for the Irish had been earned by the performance of their fearless brigades in the Civil War, while his respect for the Jews dated back to the Maccabees. When Roosevelt resigned as police commissioner in 1897 to become secretary of the navy, Grandpa and thousands of other policemen were saddened at their loss. But with the Spanish-American War imminent, it soon became apparent that their loss was the nation's gain. Having served in Roosevelt's Bike Brigade, a much maligned group of mobile cops who eventually proved their worth on the Bowery and in mid-Manhattan, Grandpa was a staunch supporter of Teddy's methods: Speak softly and carry a big stick. And Grandpa still wore on his hip the .32-caliber Colt revolver that Roosevelt had designated as the department's mandatory off-duty weapon.

When in a reflective mood, which happened more often these days, Grandpa would tell the kids about his adventures during the Manhattan streetcar strikes of July 1899, the Westside riots of 1900, and the battles he fought on the Bowery. Whenever he ran short of material, which wasn't often, he turned to the stories his father had told him about the murderous Five Points district of lower Manhattan in the 1850s or the Irish Civil War riots of 1863.

At seventy-five, his lean six-foot-five-inch frame sloped forward, so that the first thing one noticed on meeting him was his bald, well-tanned head. Despite his years, he was still a vigorous, wise man with an uncanny gift for political intrigue. It was that attribute which he hoped to exploit today to help his son. He would start at the lowest level of the police department, work his way up, and, if necessary, go outside the department. Grandpa also had a trump card he didn't want to play yet but would if he had to.

An advocate of public transportation, Grandpa used it to conduct business in the city, saving his old, brown Chevrolet for the longer trips. The dinky, a two-car train, took him to 180th Street, where he caught the cross-town bus to the Bronx police borough office; from there, he walked several blocks to the IRT express stop and took it down to Fourteenth Street. He went to police headquarters. From there, he visited the municipal building, and then he took the train back up to 180th Street, got the dinky to Dyre Avenue, and went home.

Neither the borough office, the chief inspector's office, nor the corporation counsel's office could provide him with the evidence he sought. Grandpa smiled in admiration at McGlick's thoroughness.

Detective Gibbs had been told to report to the detective borough office in the Forty-fifth Precinct, where he was to see Captain Fonnelli. The captain curtly informed Gibbs that it was policy for the detective division to cooperate with the uniformed commands, especially the division commanders, and especially Inspector McGlick. He then gave a quick dissertation on the folly of a first-grade detective like Gibbs making lieutenant's money, with no tenure and a large family to support, involving himself on the wrong side in the non-detective aspects of a case. Gibbs was getting the message but resisting it. He asked for time to think things over. Fonnelli insisted on an immediate decision.

"If you want to go back to pounding the beat at a cop's salary, that's as easy to arrange as breaking glass," Fonnelli informed him.

Gibbs was repulsed. He despised what he was hearing. He didn't like it, but before leaving the room, he got the message: He didn't see anything.

The commanding officer of the police academy, who one day would be police commissioner and unsuccessfully fight an outside investigation of widespread police corruption, requested one of his lieutenants to speak to a recruit by the name of Bill Ryan regarding reports that the young Ryan had an attitude problem.

When Ryan reported to the lieutenant's office, he received a quick lecture on what the police academy was trying to achieve; then the lieutenant got down to brass tacks.

"You're undermining what we're trying to instill in our recruits with these constant references to your father's case each time an instructor brings up the integrity issue."

"It seems to the point," Bill replied.

"Look, Ryan," the lieutenant sternly said, "you have one month to go before graduation. Either stop your comments or be dropped as a misfit."

"You're kidding," Bill said in astonishment.

"Try me," the lieutenant said, raising his voice.

"What a crock," Bill answered, shaking his head in disbelief.

The lieutenant jumped up from his chair and leaned over the desk, peering indignantly at Ryan.

"One more word and you'll be out on your ass. Did you hear that?"

"I heard," Bill said. He got up and left the room fuming.

After returning home, Grandpa placed a few phone calls then went for a leisurely stroll around the grounds, eventually extending his walk to the surrounding neighborhood. Everyone in that area of the Bronx, called Wakefield, knew him, especially the kids and senior citizens, so his unusual inquisitiveness disturbed only a few dogs. He wandered about, snooped, peeked, ambled into driveways, stopped into stores, and returned home.

It was a strange exhibition for a sober old-timer, who, at present, limited himself to two quarts of Rheingold Beer a day, but his expedition confirmed that their phone was tapped and that the source of the tap was located in the Piggly Wiggly store on the corner.

Finding the tap, Grandpa realized, had been the easy part. Now he had to decide what to do next: expose the tap, ignore it, or use it.

Later that night, after the children had gone to bed, the small group gathered in the dining room to review the implications of the day's events over coffee.

Hugh, at first, tried to exclude Margaret from these sessions, but she would have none of it.

"I'm an Irish, not Italian, wife," she said playfully.

"I'm well aware of that," Hugh replied, feigning annoyance. Sensing the sexual thrust of the remark, the others laughed.

A growing atmosphere of intrigue accompanied these discussions. The crisis had forged them into a tight-knit unit dedicated to the survival of Hugh Ryan. Tonight, their morale was exceedingly high. They knew what the enemy was doing. Bill and Grandpa related what had happened to them that day. Bill spoke first, telling them about being warned by the lieutenant to stop bringing up his father's case in class.

It was quickly agreed, three to one, that Bill should play things low key until graduation. He had a good chance at winning the Bloomingdale Trophy for having the highest academic average, but he had to be in the academy to get it. The most startling news of the evening came when Grandpa revealed the bugging operation he had uncovered. The others stared at one another wide-eyed as he reported the details. Grandpa had expected McGlick to try something like this, so he had gone looking for and uncovered the source of the tap. Margaret now mentioned she'd heard humming each time she used the phone, and Hugh commented that this meant McGlick knew about Krauss and O'Brien turning him down.

Grandpa, like any good architect, already had the framework for a new plan of attack laid out in his mind. He decided to give them the details. So, after lighting his corncob pipe and filling the air with a cloud of Sir Walter Raleigh smoke, Grandpa leaned forward, put his elbows on the table, and began to speak.

"First of all, let's face a few realities. McGlick has either closed off or will close off all our avenues of help, including Detective Gibbs." Grandpa looked at his son, who nodded acknowledgment of the inevitable.

"Let's not worry about that now," Grandpa said. "What we have to remember is that by his actions, McGlick has simply made this a case of his word versus yours. He can't manufacture witnesses from people silenced by his pressure. He's going to have enough trouble trying to keep the truth from getting out. I can't see him bringing in phony civilian witnesses, and there's a limit to how far the cops who were there that night can be pushed. They're good men who have so far been scared impotent by this guy. Can you blame them?

"At the same time, we worry McGlick. Why else would he have our phone tapped? As it now stands, with your good record over nineteen years of service and Adler in your corner, there's always a possibility the insubordination charge won't stand, even with McGlick's testimony against you. He probably knows that. Those are options he must live with unless he can stack the deck in his favor. And he will. If we were dealing with a normal superior officer, he'd probably let you cop a plea, but not McGlick.

"Now comes the hairy part. Like McGlick, I'm an old-timer. I've met this type before. If he thinks his neck is at stake, he'll stop nothing short of murder to get you. Remember, no matter what he says, he's not sure how all this will end up. Trials can be tricky. Surprises can and do happen. That could be another reason for the tap. He's looking for more information on you, an opening, an opportunity—that's why this tap must be gotten rid of. We can't afford any slips. Suppose an unknown ally calls. He would be exposed to McGlick. If I read him right, the only way he can ensure that the trial comes off right is to damage your good reputation. There's only one sure way to do that: a setup, a frame."

The others were stunned by Grandpa's conclusion. Several moments of silence passed before a confused Bill asked, "What can we do?"

Without waiting for an answer, Margaret said, "If Hugh stays out sick, they can't touch him."

"My shoulder's been acting up again," Hugh said.

"Margaret's right," Grandpa said. "You should stay out sick as long as possible."

"What kind of frame-up might they try?" Bill asked, returning to the first subject.

"It could be anything: booze, prostitutes, narcotics," Grandpa answered.

"Can we beat it?" Hugh anxiously asked.

"If and when you go back to work, you'll have to be very careful. They'll probably spring the frame at night, during a four-to-twelve or a midnight-to-eight shift. Expect a last-minute change in your assignment. They won't try this in the station house; planting contraband in lockers is passé. This will happen outside, on the street.

"If they put you in a patrol car, never take the chauffeur they assign; pick another cop, a black or Puerto Rican, if possible. McGlick won't trust them. And always keep your chauffeur with you, he's your protection. If they fail to implicate you during motor patrol, their next step will be to assign you to foot patrol, and that will be a tough one to figure a way out of."

Grandpa fell silent and carefully thought about a way around this next possible threat. Hugh and the others quietly watched, marveling at his ability to get inside enemy lines.

Finally, Grandpa emerged from his rumination seemingly without having found a solution. He shrugged and suggested that it was late and that it would be best if they all slept on it.

Grandpa already had part of the solution but knew Hugh would reject it out of hand if it were suggested now. Perhaps after Hugh returned from the police surgeon tomorrow, he would give Grandpa's idea more serious consideration.

16

WHEN THE MAN left his apartment building, Hirschel was waiting. The morning rush hour was at its height along 138ᵗʰ Street, so it was easy to follow the man to the IRT station. Once the man got onto the downtown express, Hirschel rapidly returned to the building and climbed the stairs to the fifth floor.

After knocking many times and getting no response, he used a "loid" to open the door and was into the apartment in seconds. To his surprise, the three rooms were finely decorated in a Spanish motif.

The first thing Hirschel found on searching the place was the Bible. There were two markers in it, each revealing a page with underlined words. After reading those, he put the Bible down. Hirschel knew he had his man. He had heard of the often violated, "Thou shalt not commit adultery," but the second prohibition made him chuckle. He had already forgotten the exact wording, though its intent justified even his lifestyle. "Better to seed a whore than to seed the bathroom floor," was how he smilingly paraphrased it. After finding the Bible, it did not take him long to discover the pile of linen napkins and the man's name, Raoul Guzman.

Hirschel had to laugh. While he and Davis had staked out the church for the wrong reason, Guzman, deciding to change his MO for the right reason, had walked into their trap. It was all so ironic. If the public ever found out that this was how most arrests were made, the detective mystique would crumble. Thank God for luck, he thought.

The toughest part that night at the church had been for Hirschel to convince Gordon Davis not to check Raoul out any further. Had Davis seen Raoul go down the church steps after the girl, as Hirschel did, he too would have seen through the drunk routine. After they let Raoul go, Davis returned to his church stakeout, but Hirschel was free to follow his subject and, inside of twenty minutes, knew where he lived.

Hirschel quickly put everything back where he found it, left the apartment, dropped a dime into a pay phone on the corner, dialed a number, and after a short conversation, left the area.

✻ ✻ ✻

Grandpa was certain that neither the district attorney nor a judge had approved the tap, but it would still be a problem getting rid of it. Grandpa was counting on McGlick's sense of superiority to help in that direction.

The cauldron had to be stirred, however, and that was what Grandpa undertook to do. He began making a series of phone calls. First, he complained about the wiretap to the local precinct, then the borough office, the mayor's office, and finally, he complained to the Piggly Wiggly store owner. All were informed that an illegal tap, not approved by any DA or judge, was currently being conducted from a store at 932 Dyre Avenue, indiscriminately recording all calls to and from Fairbanks 7-5336.

✻ ✻ ✻

The telephone rang once before Silent Tony picked up.

"The milk was left outside and went sour," a voice said.

"Too bad," Tony answered. "Who left it out?"

"The old man," the voice replied.

"I'll call right back," Tony answered.

He hung up and went to see McGlick. After mulling the situation over for several minutes, McGlick ordered Tony to lift the tap. "That old bastard could turn out to be dangerous, but he won't be able to stop my next blitz," McGlick snorted.

Grandpa left the house, went to the corner, and waited. Twenty minutes later, two burly men emerged from the Piggly Wiggly store carrying valises, which they put into an old white Studebaker, and drove off.

It made Grandpa feel useful again to have fathomed McGlick's devious brain, but he was too wise to gloat. It had only been a minor setback for their relentless adversary, and anyway, gloating was a fool's vice. He also knew that McGlick's next attack would be more difficult to stop.

Police Surgeon Samuels' office was located on Crotona Avenue in the Tremont section of the Bronx, a predominantly Jewish and Italian area. For a quarter century, the doctor had provided thousands of cops with the best medical advice and care possible, as good as that offered to his private patients.

Dr. Samuels was the exception to the rule that a police surgeon did not give a damn about the problems of the cops who came to see him. They often treated them instead with disdain.

One reason this irritated cops was that these surgeons worked only a few hours each week, collecting a captain's salary and doing little to earn it. A second reason was that a tacit agreement was in force between surgeons and the top police brass. The administrators wouldn't recommend abolishment of the expensive surgeon system as long as the doctors recommended these top officials for benefits such as tax-free, three-quarter-pay disability pensions when their retirement came around.

Samuels, a heart specialist by training, unlike most of the other surgeons, was a doctor first and a bureaucrat second.

Hugh told the doctor how he had been under tremendous pressure lately and found himself tiring easily. After a comprehensive examination that included a cardiogram, Samuels announced that Hugh was fine. He then ordered a prescription of rest and relaxation for his patient.

"By the way," Dr. Samuels said, "are you aware you have a friend downtown?" He was indirectly informing Hugh that there had been inquiries and instructions about him.

Hugh nodded and answered, "I figured I might have."

Samuels then asked when Ryan's last tour fell and ordered him back to work just after it ended. With two days off following the last tour, the doctor had provided Hugh with a couple of extra days of rest. Ryan thanked the doctor and returned home.

Samuels then called the chief surgeon and told him how he had handled the Ryan matter. The chief surgeon chewed him out. Samuels listened with indifference to the lecture and warning. When the chief surgeon finished, Samuels issued his own warning. "This man is an incipient heart case. Tell headquarters that. If they continue harassing him, he'll wind up with a massive coronary."

✻ ✻ ✻

McDarby's was a pleasant Second Avenue pub in the east seventies of Manhattan catering mostly to a sports crowd and a sprinkling of actors and detectives. The owner, Ted McDarby, often proclaimed the latter two were interchangeable.

Just after twelve noon, Hirschel entered McDarby's and took a corner booth to wait for the man with the money, the man he had called that morning once he was sure about Raoul.

He had heard through the grapevine, as had other "hungry" detectives, that there was a grand in it for the guy who pedigreed the rapist without arresting him. It had been rumored the Brooklyn mob put up the money. Some conjectured that one of the victims had been a mobster's girl. They figured that the man pointed out as the rapist would be rubbed out, and therefore, many wouldn't touch the case. Hirschel was one of those who didn't care; a grand was a grand. If the rapist was hit, he was only getting what he deserved.

Hirschel had come from a fine Orthodox Jewish family in Brooklyn. Being the only son—he had three sisters—and the first cop in the family, his choice of careers disturbed his mother. His grandfather, Simon, however, a tailor's apprentice who in his youth had fought in the Budapest ghetto uprising, encouraged the Americanization of his grandson. He wanted a Jacobian man, a tough, righteous individual ready and willing to fight injustice. Hirschel's father had died years before in a trolley accident so a special bond had developed between Simon and his grandson. They would spend hours walking in Prospect Park talking about religion, the world, and sports, especially the Dodgers, the Brooklyn Bums. As time passed, Simon noticed some minor changes in his grandson, the cop. He had moved to Manhattan and visited less often. But as Simon often said to Alfred's mother, "Everyone is entitled to lead his own life."

Al's mother was bothered that he never married, blaming it on the crazy hours he worked as a policeman. "You should have gone to college and got a profession," she would tell him.

He would just say, "I'm happy, Mama. I'm okay."

Hirschel had been an honest cop but had fallen into bad company when he made detective. He got the gold shield after having been wounded capturing a robber who had killed a Brooklyn storeowner. He spent three years in a Midtown-Manhattan squad before his transfer to the Bronx due to a botched shakedown attempt. The move uptown had cost him heavily in terms of lost pads and scores. The rapist caper was his first decent score in months. He hadn't wanted to pass it up, although he had some reservations about it. In Manhattan, the pad was automatic and the scores easy. A fight in a bar became a fight in the street; a property felony arrest became a misdemeanor arrest. It was all so smooth: the broads, the loft, the trips, the Manhattan nightlife. It demanded cash, but that was always rolling in. Now he had to scratch for everything. If he wanted to continue his Manhattan lifestyle, he had to—and he would.

Before long, Silent Tony entered McDarby's, dapper in a blue sharkskin suit and wearing a black fedora with a small red feather in the band. With a nod, he slid next to the detective, and both ordered drinks then talked a bit. Finally, they got down to business.

Tony looked around and then slipped a bulging white envelope to Hirschel. The envelope disappeared quickly into the vest pocket of Hirschel's sport jacket. No sooner had the first one vanished than Tony put another of the same size on the table. Hirschel's eyes lit up and rolled as he reached for it, but Tony held it firmly.

"Make sure that the rapist don't hit again—for five more days," said Tony. "Here's another grand for you."

"Ain't bad," said Hirschel, looking at the envelope.

"Any questions?" Tony asked.

"Not from me," said Hirschel, grinning and reaching for the envelope.

Tony slid the envelope over to him. It went into the other vest pocket.

Tony looked intently into Hirschel's dark-brown eyes.

"Don't blow it, kid; my boss would be very upset."

It was McGlick who had insisted that the rapist be watched until Adler was out. McGlick had his own code, and it didn't include allowing rapists to roam free.

Tony didn't wait for Hirschel to respond. He just got up and walked out. Everything I heard about that kid is true, he thought, glad to be out of his company. He'd put his head in a toilet for a buck and what's worse, never ask why. Sooner or later, he's going to cause a lot of grief. An uneasy feeling suddenly overtook Tony.

*   *   *

An hour after Hugh returned from Dr. Samuels' office, feeling surprisingly well, he received a call from the Two-one. The roll-call man confirmed that Hugh was, indeed, returned from sick leave as of 8:00 AM on the twenty-first. Hugh sensed the man was about to say something he didn't want to say.

"Your squad has been changed again," he finally announced in a rush of words. "You're in the Fifteenth and have to do a 4:00 PM to midnight shift on the twenty-first."

"This is a lot of crap!" Ryan yelled. "I'm entitled to two days off after my set of tours even if I've been out sick. What's Stevens pulling?" He was angry, upset, and could feel his face flushing red and his neck growing stiff.

"Hey, Sarge, this isn't my idea," the roll-call man explained sympathetically.

"The bastards, they're backing me up against the wall!" Ryan yelled, losing control of himself. Margaret heard the outburst from the kitchen and sighed deeply.

"I'm sorry," the roll-call man replied. "Stevens told me to tell you if you complained, that you will be credited with two days on the books. The sergeants' delegate was complaining to him about the time you lost when you transferred in."

"I asked him to," said Ryan.

"Yeah, well, sorry, Sarge. See you on the twenty-first." The roll-call man hung up.

"Sure," Hugh replied into the humming phone, "I'll see you too." He hung up, knowing that when the next transfer came, his new CO would inform him he didn't honor lost time from previous commands.

Hugh, inside a box with collapsing sides, had to remain calm and brace himself for the constant shocks. The best way to do that, he decided, was to take a nap for the next few hours.

The family meeting that night was subdued. It seemed as if they were battling an enormous octopus. Each time they chopped off an arm, another replaced it. Their enthusiasm waned as they contemplated the enormity of the task ahead of them. It was particularly frustrating for Hugh, being kept off balance, not knowing from which direction the next blow would come or how severe it would be.

Sensing the futility of the battle, Margaret made an extraordinary suggestion, "Quit, Hugh. Just walk away from this." The men were not receptive to her call for surrender.

"Margaret," Hugh said, slightly irritated. "I've over one hundred fifty thousand dollars invested in that pension. I'm not just going to throw it away. That's crazy."

Grandpa affirmed the position, and Bill echoed, "He's right, Ma."

Bill, young, strong, and impervious to the scalding psychological torments surrounding him, urged even stronger and more reckless actions: picket headquarters or go to the newspapers.

Hugh, the traditionalist, angrily squashed that. Somewhere in the police code, it read, "It is improper to go public with internal police problems." Grandpa, the pragmatist, remained silent. He had already violated the code that morning with his phone calls.

Once again, it was Grandpa who put fire to the wet kindling, put their struggle into perspective, and outlined the strategy of their next series of moves.

"Look," he told the others, "overall, it hasn't been such a bad day. We know Dr. Samuels is a fair man. That's critical. We may need him later. Okay, so someone downtown overruled him and had your squad changed to negate the rest he wanted for you. There's more to this than their wanting to demoralize you." He paused, looking at each of them like a lawyer staring at the jury before setting them up for the clincher.

"They've already picked a date and an alternate date; the frame-up is on this set of four-to-twelves."

Holding his hand up to stifle comments and questions, he continued, "There are other forces at work here than just McGlick. I don't know who they are, but this has something to do with the Seventh Division. McGlick had to receive the support of a heavyweight downtown to initiate this organizational kill. We can rule out Atmont, so if anyone downtown okayed this, you can be sure he's getting a favor in return from McGlick. Do we all agree on that?"

"It sounds logical to me," Hugh answered, glancing at the others. "It might also be helpful if we found out who's helping McGlick and what favor he might do in return."

"You're right, Hugh," Grandpa answered, "but leave that for later. Let's deal with first things first. This morning, I successfully eliminated the tap on our phone. Tactically, this was critical for us. I'll explain why in a minute. Remember how I outlined a possible frame scenario last night?" He looked at each of them, and they nodded. "Well, if they can't get Hugh while he's on motor patrol duty, they'll try it during foot patrol. Or they may not try the patrol car tactic. They may send you out on foot patrol first. If at all possible, don't go. Unfortunately, I'm sure they'll have Captain Stevens work it so you'll have to go out on the street. If so, you'll need our help. There's where the phone comes in, which is why it was essential to lift the tap.

"Once you're out of the station house, go to the nearest phone booth and give us a call. Though I'm positive the tap has been removed, we must assume it's still there, so use the phrase 'Wait for me' to indicate you're going on the street. We'll need twenty-five minutes to reach you, so you'll have to kill close to half an hour. I'll leave the 'how' up to you. By then, Bill and I will be in the area to cover you in our brown Chevy."

"I don't know," Hugh replied. "Do you really think they'll try this?"

"We went over that last night," Grandpa wearily said. "It's a certainty. McGlick will play to win. How strong his need to win will determine the kind of frame he'll try. Never forget that."

When he said this, Grandpa's lower lip began to quiver. The strain was beginning to show on him too. Though still strong, he was slowly being enervated by their uncertainty and doubt. In a battle of this kind, he was the only man who could pull them through. He knew that, and it worried him. I hope I can last to the end of this, thought the old man. By God, I have to, he told himself.

17

POLICE COMMISSIONER O'Grady, returning to headquarters from the mayor's office, was in a bad humor. He rushed through the revolving front door from the sidewalk into the lobby and swung right toward the waiting private elevator. The security sergeant had the brown-grained lift ready.

A quick "Thanks, Jake" from the commissioner and the old machine jerked upward.

If it wasn't one person or group complaining, the commissioner thought, it was four or five somebody elses: the cardinal, the Fifth Avenue business association, a black group in Brooklyn, a white group in Queens. It had been that kind of day.

The cardinal had been in a rage—a street prostitute was using his confessional for her oral tricks. She would sit in the priest's box in the middle, her patrons on either side, and perform her deviant acts through the opening used to hear confession. O'Grady laughed, thinking about how it had come to the cardinal's attention. He had opened the sliding voice door one afternoon to do his duty and a bulging circumcised penis was thrust into his face.

The president of the Fifth Avenue association was complaining about some nut who was firing pellets from a CO_2 gun through jewelry store windows.

A minister from a black group in Brooklyn wanted more black cops in their neighborhood.

A rabbi from a white group in Queens wanted more cops, period. The playful rabbi then asked the cardinal why he had emphasized the sculptured nature of the penis—was he suggesting a Jewish plot against him? The cardinal told the rabbi that he would show him something after the meeting which would prove conclusively that many Christians had adopted their Jewish brothers' ways. Several others at the meeting agreed to do likewise. The mayor asked O'Grady to join the group. O'Grady declined when a reporter asked for a photo session of the demonstration.

Chief Inspector Yates had received O'Grady's call from the mayor's office, and as they talked, he made notations of dossiers to be pulled and updated, topics to be researched, and reports to be prepared. As directed, he was waiting in the commissioner's office upon his arrival.

The mayor had thrown an unusual amount of junk at O'Grady today, thought Yates. More secure city administrators distilled out minor items and forgot them. But O'Grady was new; he still hadn't gotten the hang of dealing with the mayor. Until he did, everything would be important.

They had covered several items when O'Grady said, "I got one here I forgot to mention: Cop in the Bronx claims his phone is being tapped by Inspector McGlick. Do you know about that?"

Yates's bad leg began to shake uncontrollably.

"What's wrong?" asked a concerned O'Grady.

"Damn leg," said the unnerved Yates. "It will be okay in a minute." Yates struggled to his feet. "Just have to stretch it." I can't believe this, Yates thought. Is O'Grady setting me up? He glanced at O'Grady out of the corner of his eye. The guy seems upset by my attack. But who the hell knows?

O'Grady was smiling. "There's no one as paranoid as a paranoid cop," he said. "The mayor told me that, Chief."

Yates was really tense now. "What do you mean, Commissioner?"

"The old guy in the Bronx, of course," said the grinning commissioner. "The mayor must think it's important somehow."

"Yeah, right, boss," said Yates. "I better check that out right away." He limped toward the door.

McGlick smiled upon recognizing Yates's voice on the line. The smile quickly vanished. Yates's words had that faint, disembodied character which told McGlick that something, somewhere was not kosher.

"Inspector McGlick, I'd like to see you downtown."

McGlick nervously licked his lips. "Is it about anything you can mention now, Chief?"

"It's too detailed to go into now," Yates answered. "I want to see you in person. Be in my office in a half-hour."

"Sure, Chief. I'll be there as soon as possible." As McGlick hung up the phone and reached for his hat, he felt the hairs on the back of his neck bristle. What the hell went wrong? he wondered.

Half an hour later, McGlick found himself in Yates's mahogany-paneled office occupying an uncomfortable high-backed, red leather chair in front of Yates's desk. He was waiting for Yates to speak. What's he waiting for, thought McGlick, a confession? Fuck him. I'm bending my principles for only one reason: Ryan. If it wasn't for that, I'd turn the chisler over to the DA.

Yates sat there staring at the fidgety McGlick. I was told I'd have trouble controlling the bastard, thought Yates. But his price is right—it always has been. There's enough fingers in the pie anyway.

"I saw the PC today, Terence," he said distantly. "He knows about your tap."

Yates fell silent and watched the words sink in. McGlick's mouth fell open.

"Why didn't I know about this, Terence?" he said coldly.

"I've already killed it," said McGlick defensively. "How did the mayor find out?"

"The old man, Terence," said Yates. "He called the mayor's office."

"That bastard—I'll get him," said McGlick, venom in his words.

Yates sat forward. "It's Adler we're after, Terence, then Hugh Ryan. Remember? Ignore the old man!" he said, raising his voice ever so slightly.

"What did you tell the mayor, Chief?"

"That I was looking into the matter," said Yates. "Officially, that's why you're here, Terence. I'm investigating."

Yates's frozen words sent a chill through McGlick. Yates watched McGlick's eyes. Yates smiled; he knew what McGlick was thinking.

"They don't call me the 'Shadow' for nothing, Terence. Everything I do is covered. I'm there, but I'm not there. Do you understand?"

"Yeah, right, Chief," said McGlick, suddenly afraid that Yates was backing away from him.

"Don't worry, Terence. I'm making an exception for you in this case—I'll cover you."

McGlick didn't respond. Yeah, thought McGlick, you're making an exception—you're making exceptionally big bucks. Don't try to bullshit me. You're running for your life. The next purge of the chiefs is only a few months away. Exceptions—bullshit. Cover me—you bet your ass you will.

"Now," said Yates, his voice suddenly gaining substance, "let's get our game plan together."

"Right," said McGlick, subdued but still annoyed.

"Adler is first," said Yates. "He's your ticket to chief, Terence. So sit on this Ryan thing until Adler is out on the twenty-fourth, okay?" He didn't wait for a reply. "By the way, Dr. Samuels claims that Ryan will have a heart attack if we don't leave off."

"Damn doctor," said McGlick. "He's always bellyaching. Ryan's a big bastard—strong as a horse—nothing's going to hurt him." McGlick tapped his own chest to emphasize the point. He then tapped his head. "If he can't take the pressure, let him quit."

"I ordered him back to work anyway," said Yates, struggling to his feet, his face contorted as he stretched his withered leg. These Ryans really drive this guy wild, thought Yates. I don't like it. He jumps into third gear with the mention of the Ryan name. Yates decided to reinforce his position.

"Terence," he said evenly, "I've put the power of my office behind you for one reason: You're doing me a favor with Adler. Whatever you do on Ryan from now on had better be damned foolproof. If there's a scandal, I'll fall too. And if I go, Terence, you can be damn sure you will too. Is that clear?"

McGlick nodded, trying to control his anger, his face as white as mutton lard.

"Okay, now that that's understood," said Yates, "what's with Ryan? Tell me everything, and I mean everything. What else besides the tap don't I know about?"

"I've been doing plenty," said McGlick roughly. "I've shut off his witnesses. I've made sure he has nothing on me. All he's got now is his reputation and Adler as a character witness. I can't stop Adler from testifying, but before I'm finished, Ryan's reputation will be so tainted even Jack the Ripper wouldn't take the knife to him."

Yates smiled at McGlick's words. "What'd you do, Terence, try the stolen watches or marijuana in the locker routine? You know where that will get you."

"It's worked before," said McGlick, bothered by the putdown.

"You just said it, Terence," said Yates instructively, his voice cold and even. "It has worked so many times before that it's now easily recognized as a frame." Yates walked to the western window and looked out across the city. What a beautiful city, he thought. And I have to spend my time with a Neanderthal. Well, not much longer. He worked his way to his chair and dropped into it.

McGlick, restless and upset, waited for Yates to continue.

"Terence," said Yates clinically, his pea-green eyes fixed on McGlick's nose, "I've destroyed many enemies. Halfway measures suck. They don't work. When they're on the ground, drive the blade through into the earth. That way, they can't get up. The Ryans are floored. Don't go to a goddamn neutral corner. Bludgeon them into extinction. It's that simple, Terence. It's the professional way. It's the way all good chiefs operate. Do you understand that, Terence?"

Yates had not once raised his voice. Yet McGlick could feel the words cut through him like a dentist's drill on an exposed nerve.

"I see your point, Chief," he replied, sensing his own jeopardy for the first time.

"Make your plans, Terence," Yates told him. "Use any of my people you need. But remember—each is only to be told what he needs to know."

"Right, I understand," said McGlick.

"Do it in the Two-one," Yates continued. "It's the safest place. I don't want the particulars either, but do it right. Understand?"

McGlick nodded, anxious to leave and get some fresh air.

"One more reminder, Terence," said Yates, standing for their farewell. "Take no action on Ryan until the twenty-fourth. After Adler's out, you can have your fun."

"Don't worry, Chief," said McGlick, shaking Yates's clammy hand, "Adler will be out of the Three-nine by midnight of the twenty-fourth." McGlick left.

McGlick sighed upon reaching the street. He took a deep breath. Why the hell do I have to wait on Ryan? he thought. It still didn't make sense to him. Oh well, he decided, if the chief wants it that way and nothing upsets our plans, why not?

18

BILL'S COMMENTS the night before about going to the papers and Hugh's rejoinder were bothering Grandpa. He wondered if Hugh was right about not going public. Maybe he had gone too far to exorcise the tap. Today, he planned an even more radical step, a visit to an honest DA.

Sitting at the kitchen table, spooning up cornflakes and bananas for lunch, Grandpa searched his encyclopedic memory for something that disturbed him. He finally located the date, filed under 1912.

A Tenderloin gambling house operator, Herman Rosenthal, had complained to the newspapers and the Manhattan DA that he was the victim of police shakedowns. Rosenthal had violated the code by ratting and going public. A short time later, he was shot dead on the steps of the Metropole Hotel at Forty-third Street and Broadway.

The Manhattan DA avenged the scandalous killing. There were five Sing Sing executions. Lefty Louis, Gyp the Blook, Whitey Lewis, Dago Frank, and Police Lieutenant Charles Becker, head of the Tenderloin district vice squad, went to the electric chair.

He had gone to the papers and the DA, broken the code, and been murdered; it all played itself over and over in Grandpa's mind. He grimaced but then shook it off. What the hell? This wasn't 1912. If anything, he thought, Becker's execution for murdering Rosenthal made cops realize the folly of getting involved in murder. Realizing that it had taken him a few minutes to remember the case, he decided, just to be on the safe side, to send a Photostat of the front page of the

Daily News from the day Lieutenant Becker was executed to McGlick, anonymously of course. He didn't think McGlick would try to kill Hugh, but just to make sure, he would send the Photostat anyway. Grandpa smiled. It had a nice touch to it.

Hugh would have objected had he known Grandpa was going to the district attorney. Hugh felt this was an in-house battle. Grandpa believed it was another exercise in futility, but there was no room for assumptions where direct evidence was remotely possible.

The DA's office was in the courthouse on Grand Concourse and 161st Street in the Bronx, diagonally across from the fashionable Concourse Plaza Hotel. Even the Yankees stayed in the Concourse Plaza when they played in town. The Fahertys had reserved the ballroom there for the following fourth of May; Bill Ryan had given his fiancée, Mary, an engagement ring at the Standard Athletic Club's Westchester softball championship dinner at the Glen Island Casino. She was a beautiful girl, he thought, and from such a fine, pub-owning Irish family too.

The wisteria and crabapple trees were in full bloom in John Mullaly Park adjacent to the courthouse. Looking at them, Grandpa, a park-bencher for years, decided to give his bald dome ten minutes in the warm afternoon sun before continuing on to his destination.

After several minutes, he seemed suddenly to fall asleep. His sonorous breathing disturbed the other bench occupant, who moved.

A short time later, Grandpa awoke with a slight headache and a stiff leg; he attributed this to the sun. He didn't realize at the time that he had suffered a slight stroke. In a few minutes, fully recovered, he was on his way to the DA's office.

Grandpa knew he had to be delicate in his approach to the Democratic DA, for it had been rumored he was easily offended by Republicans. The arsenal available to back Grandpa's appeal were his age, his background, a cold logical outrage concerning his son's case, and a sincere appeal to the DA's basic integrity.

Grandpa got past the receptionist easily. The first-grade detective was tough.

"Let me get this straight," said the detective. "You want to see the DA about a barroom killing in which your son had a fight with Inspector McGlick and you want to speak to the prisoner, too?"

"That's right," said Grandpa, "and I'm a Republican, too."

The detective gave Grandpa his "another head case" smile.

"He'll see me," said Grandpa. "Check it out."

The detective did. The DA agreed to give Grandpa two minutes. The detective escorted Grandpa down a marble-floored hallway to a door. The sign read "Interrogation Room." They entered. It was a large room with a high ceiling, empty except for two wooden chairs facing each other—one at the north wall, one at the south wall. The DA was sitting in the one to the south. Grandpa took the north chair; the sun coming through the shadeless window blinded him.

Grandpa began to chuckle. "My God," said Grandpa, "if this is the way you treat a Republican, I feel sorry for the crooks."

The DA burst out laughing and said, "Okay, Mr. Ryan, you passed the nut test."

The detective shrugged and frowned as if to say, "So I thought this guy belonged in a cracker factory? Sue me." The DA led Grandpa into his plush office.

Dominick Broglio, a short, pudgy Italian, was sympathetic to Grandpa's crisp, valid arguments, but reality kept surfacing. Broglio's office needed the staff of detectives provided by the police department to maintain its investigative effectiveness. So a suggestion from a high-ranking detective boss to allow the perpetrator of a low-level homicide to cop a plea served two important ends. First, and most important, it avoided the exhaustive work and considerable expense required to prepare for and then conduct a subsequent trial. Secondly, it ensured the future good will and cooperation of the Bronx police hierarchy.

Broglio explained that in good conscience, he couldn't renege on a deal he had made and now threaten the prisoner with a trial unless he told the truth about the nightstick incident. Both Legal Aid and the police would be furious if he reversed himself on that basis. Anyway, Broglio reasoned, Ryan just didn't have the political clout to offset that kind of flack.

Broglio tried to be as fair as possible under the circumstances. While Grandpa waited, the DA called Legal Aid and explained the situation. An agreement was reached to allow Grandpa to interview the prisoner later that afternoon in the presence of the prisoner's lawyer.

"If you can convince the both of them to go along with a trial," Broglio said, "I've no choice but to go along. To be honest with you, if the man agreed to your proposal, he'd either be a fool or an idealist, and I'm sure he's neither."

The interview went about as Broglio and Grandpa expected. The prisoner, realizing good fortune had dealt him a blackjack hand of twenty, most certainly wasn't going to draw another card.

"Man, with this plea, I'll be out in three years," the black man said.

With nothing to lose, Grandpa tried one of his hurt looks on the inmate.

"Man, look at me any way you want, it won't help. Why should I take chances? I'm only talking to you out of respect for your son. But, pops, believe me, I'm not saying a word. They fry niggers in this state, man. Haven't you heard? They'd fry my nigger ass for the fun of it. No, sir, I'm no roasting chicken. You'd better believe that." Grandpa believed it.

McGlick's tough, thought Grandpa as he boarded the bus. He got a deal for the prisoner so he couldn't talk. Couldn't talk? The guy would be an idiot if he did. Grandpa realized that he had only one legitimate move left.

It didn't take long before McGlick got the news. The old man had made another attempt to pierce the cover-up. McGlick was frantic, this coming on top of his recent visit with Yates. He had to get Hugh Ryan and spook the old buzzard before their maligning stories reached the wrong circles. He decided to move immediately and devastatingly, even if the chief inspector objected. To his surprise, Yates agreed that immediate action was required. A strategy meeting was set up for that afternoon. Ryan would be hit tomorrow night.

IT WAS A DECISION Grandpa didn't want to make. He had avoided it for over fifty years. But now was the time. If he waited much longer, they would be so engulfed in McGlick's quicksand that extrication would be impossible. Even with his trump card, Grandpa knew the best to be hoped for was a stabilized situation which still favored McGlick.

As twilight fell, Grandpa guided his old Chevy over the Whitestone Bridge and headed east toward Merrick, Long Island, along the Belt Parkway.

It seemed a short drive as he debated the propriety of the present attack. Then, as he pulled up in front of Don Trataglia's family compound, he knew he was doing the right thing. Grandpa removed his holstered .32-caliber Colt and put it under the front seat.

Then he got out of the car. He pulled out his wallet and took out a tiny packet which was wrapped in cellophane and held in place by rubber bands. He removed the rubber bands as he approached the two guards at the opening in the wall which circled the Trataglia estate.

Before they could challenge him, he held out a yellowed card and said, "I'd like to see the don. Please give this to him."

The guard who took the card looked it over quizzically, shrugged, then said, "Okay, wait here."

In the darkness, the only thing Grandpa could see beyond the wall was the huge outline of a scalloped tile roof reflecting the light of the August moon.

When the guard returned, he motioned Grandpa inside the wall and passed him on to two companions. Grandpa now saw two houses—a Moorish type with a tile roof and a huge English Tudor covered with ivy. After a meticulous search, for which Trataglia's men apologized, he was led through a garden to the side door of the columned Tudor mansion and into a teak-furnished office with flowered, red velvet wallpaper.

The don, a dark, distinguished-looking man in his late sixties, attired in slacks and a sports shirt open at the neck, closed the roll-top desk he stood at. "Please sit down," he said, as he studied the stooped giant who had entered the room.

Grandpa moved toward a straight-backed chair. The don waved the bodyguards out. "You stay here, Joey," he said to another man, his son.

The don then sat down in an oversized leather chair behind the large desk, clasped his hands together on the desk, and waited for Grandpa to state his business.

"Mr. Trataglia," Grandpa began in a respectful but strong tone, "my name is John Ryan, John Brendan Ryan. I'm a retired New York City patrolman. I had—"

Before Grandpa could continue, the don held up a hand and interrupted him. He then broke into a smile as he rose from his chair and offered Grandpa his hand. "The years have been kind to you, Patrolman Ryan. You know I'm a Trataglia, but yet you do not recognize me."

"You're not Mario?" Grandpa asked incredulously, as he shook the don's hand warmly.

"That's right. You assumed young Mario would never amount to anything. Perhaps you thought this don had to be one of the other five brothers, or even a cousin."

He didn't give Grandpa time to respond as it wasn't his intent to embarrass his visitor. "Joey, come here. I want you to meet an honest cop, excuse me, patrolman." Joey was obviously confused by this.

"Joey is my youngest son. He knows nothing about my father and how you came to possess a Trataglia business card with my father's signature on it." Turning to Joey, he said, "Pour us some vino."

"If you'd like, I'll tell your son the story of our first meeting, Mario—excuse me, I mean Don Trataglia."

The don playfully interrupted. "You still don't let anything slide, do you?" Trataglia's infectious laughter had Grandpa chuckling too.

Joey was surprised. He hadn't seen his father so animated in years. Whoever this Ryan was, his father had great affection for the man.

"As I was saying," Grandpa continued, "if you'd like, I can tell your son about us."

"Please do. You're a guest in my house, and it would be rude of me to deny such a small request." The don well remembered Ryan's penchant for storytelling.

Joey appreciated the ancient game being played out and waited with interest for the story to begin.

Before starting, Grandpa peeled open a fresh dollar Tiamo cigar. The don signaled his approval and said, "You haven't done badly for an honest man." Joey pulled his chair closer to the Irishman. Grandpa smiled, lit the cigar, blew out a circle of smoke, and began his tale.

"I first met your grandfather, Bruno, in 1903, shortly after his arrival in New York. Bruno was a good family man with six sons, three daughters, an incredibly attractive wife, Marie, and a dog named Liberty. He was ambitious and soon opened a small shop on Mott Street just north of Canal. The family lived in a large fourth-floor apartment near the store.

"On several occasions, the youngest son, Mario," Grandpa paused for effect, and the don snickered playfully, "was apprehended on Canal Street by a Bowery bike patrolman named Ryan while committing, let's say, an assortment of minor infractions of the law. In accordance with accepted police procedures of the time, I escorted him to his residence where rehabilitation, in the form of a stick, took place. It didn't take long before the family adopted me and I adopted them."

At this point, Trataglia interrupted to provide some perspective.

"It was the attraction of the opposites, Joey. Patrolman Ryan was always smiling, irreverent toward appeals to authority, wore his emotions on his shirt sleeves, and took everything personally if it affected him or a friend. My father, on the other hand, was always serious, respectful of authority, quiet, and separated his business from his personal views." The don fell silent and now allowed Grandpa to continue.

"It was a warm July night in 1905. I stopped off at your grandfather's apartment, as I did every Wednesday night, to enjoy Marie's pasta. She insisted on that, even though your grandfather was working late at the store. There was no hanky-panky with your grandmother, either," said Grandpa. Joey smiled at his father.

"Well, after supper, on my way back to my Bowery post, I decided to stop off at Bruno's store. Bruno and Mario had been working there alone when suddenly a squat Italian they had never seen before entered and, without a word, pulled out a .32-caliber revolver and shot them both in the legs. Drawing a second gun, he signaled to a butcher squad waiting outside: two men carrying machetes." Grandpa flicked an ash and continued.

"As the Black Hand executioners entered, Bruno and Mario, writhing in pain on the floor, recoiled in horror. It was at that moment that I jauntily entered and saw what was happening. With trembling hands and on reflex action alone, I pulled out my revolver and fired at the would-be killers.

"They fled out a rear door, but not before the squat assassin fired two shots from his reserve pistol. Not at me, but at Bruno and Mario. Then he fled, taking three of my bullets with him.

"Despite his wounds, the assassin's aim was true. He got both Bruno and Mario. Bruno begged me to save the boy. Picking Mario up, I put the moaning lad over my shoulder and carried him six blocks to the Canal Street infirmary." Grandpa took a sip of wine.

"I then raced back for Bruno, who upon learning that Mario was safe, smiled, handed me a business card with his signature on the back, redeemable at 'A life, for a life,' he said, and slumped over dead, still clutching my hand."

The don shook his head. "Even after all these years, I still tremble at the thought of that night. Of course, I was only a boy then," he quickly added. "Later that night," the don continued, "the Trataglia brothers decided to take the neighborhood from the Black Hand. It worked. We protected our business and the entire block and revenged my father's murder. That was the beginning of what you see now." He held out his arms as if to encompass the entire estate and all the enterprises he owned and bossed.

"So that's how you received the scars on your stomach," Joey said. "Every time I ask Mama about it, she just shushes me."

Without answering his son, Trataglia looked at Grandpa and said, "Enough of the old times. You came here on business. You wish to redeem this card?" he asked, pointing with two fingers of his left hand at the card on his desk.

"Yes, as I once saved your father's son, I now ask for your help in saving my son."

"It will be done, a life for a life, if that is your wish."

"No. I can't ask that, even though I wish I could."

"I would have been disappointed if you had," said the don, "though you have every right to do so. The Trataglia family has long followed your career, but after you retired, we lost track of you. Though dishonest policemen better serve our needs, we have always considered you a very special person, a brother, if you like. Today, you made me a teenager again. I'm glad you didn't destroy for me lifelong recollections of a smiling, honest young Irishman. What is it you want me to do?"

Grandpa quickly outlined the urgency of Hugh's plight and told about the forces working against him.

Trataglia listened then said, "Your son feels the mob is somehow involved, but doesn't know where the interest lies, is that right?" Grandpa nodded.

"I heard nothing about this at the last council meeting," said the don with a frown. "It must be a personal matter. It had better be."

He looked sternly at Joey. Harlem and the South Bronx were their territory. Any criminal enterprises there needed his approval. It was particularly distressing to Trataglia that an old friend had to be the one to inform him of the matter and was also scheduled to be one of the victims of the unknown venture.

"You will be contacted tomorrow," the don said. He then told Joey, "You stay here. I'll have some work for you tonight." His son nodded.

Trataglia then walked Grandpa from the office to the front gate, exchanging pleasant banter with him, a sign of respect not lost on the godfather's security detail.

THE TENSION WAS overwhelming the next morning as the Ryans breakfasted silently at the kitchen table. My bones tell me it's tonight, thought Grandpa. With all the noise I've made, they'll want this out of the way—it can only cause them problems. Grandpa still wasn't sure who "they" were. But he was sure that bigger things than Hugh Ryan were at stake here. He realized that the final decision on Hugh was weeks away in front of a dignified forum at headquarters, but tonight's guerrilla action would largely decide Hugh's fate. They could not assure victory tonight, but a poor performance meant eventual defeat. So when the phone rang, everyone anxiously twitched. Grandpa was sure the call was for him. But when Margaret answered it, she pointed to Hugh; it was the department's defense attorney.

The defense attorney, a mediocre sergeant named Kahn, had passed the bar exam on his third try four years earlier. The fact that the defendant, complainant, defense attorney, prosecutor, and trial judge all worked for the police department caused many, including Grandpa, to view it as a kangaroo court. Grandpa at first insisted Hugh hire a private lawyer. With sound logic, Hugh decided against doing that. He knew that in controversial cases, the court found as it was directed to by the police commissioner or one of his top aides. The appearance of an outside lawyer would foster the "We have to win this one" routine, which made justice even more remote. Hugh believed an outside lawyer would be disastrous, that was, until he spoke with Kahn.

Kahn said he had reviewed the case, conferred with his associates in the advocate's office, even discussed the case with several top chiefs, and concluded that the best thing for Ryan to do was to plead guilty and throw himself on the mercy of the court.

"If I plead guilty, what's their offer?" Hugh asked.

"No offer, you just have to take your chances."

Hugh was stunned. "What kind of goddamn lawyer are you?" he shouted, his voice cracking. "They want a guilty plea with no deal. Dammit, I'm willing to plead, but you're offering me nothing in return."

"That's my advice," Kahn answered.

"Well, you know what you can do with it," Hugh said, his face ashen white by now. Grandpa stepped up to the phone and tried to get Hugh's attention.

"Tell him to hold on a second," Grandpa repeatedly said. Hugh finally did so. In a whisper, Grandpa said, "Tell Kahn to try and work out a better deal. Let him know you're upset and sorry you got excited. I'll explain." Hugh nodded, said what Grandpa asked him to, then slammed the phone down into its cradle.

"That bastard is working for the other side," Hugh reported, his anger rising.

"I know," Grandpa answered, "but our only hope is a deal. If you plead innocent, make charges against McGlick that can't be proved, they'll hang you. But that's not why Kahn called. Today's special. They're testing, probing to find out if you suspect anything, and at the same time, harassing you. And your reaction was perfect. Your anger was instinctive, sincere, and straightforward. Whoever Kahn reports to will be crowing wildly, figuring you'll be birdseed tonight."

Grandpa saw a flicker of doubt in Hugh's eyes. "Believe me, son," said Grandpa grabbing Hugh's arm, "what was speculation is now a certainty."

Hugh nodded, slumped down into an armchair, stroked his chin, and then thought about the unpleasant night that lay ahead and the trap he had to walk into. Grandpa used the interval of silence to repeat his instructions on what tactics Hugh was to employ. Then, he cryptically added that other help had been secured. Hugh's persistent questions about this help went unanswered. All Grandpa would say was, "If someone says he's trying to help, believe him."

Hugh was on the roof cementing back a few loose chimney bricks to relax his nerves. Margaret had gone to the Nativity School to pay September's monthly tuition in advance. Bill was taking his next-to-last academic test at the police academy. Grandpa waited impatiently for the phone to ring. The call came a bit after eleven.

"Drive to Ferry Point Park now," the voice on the phone said. "Park under the Whitestone Bridge. Wait in the car." Grandpa hung up, got the car, and drove to the southeast Bronx.

After parking, he didn't wait long. A familiar figure came to the passenger side of the car and knocked on the window. When Joey saw the button was up, he opened the door and slid in next to Grandpa.

"Hi, Joey. How're we doing?"

"Menza-menza," Joey answered with a smile. "The don was impressed, sir—you were right, it's definitely going down tonight."

Grandpa grinned. He was matching McGlick step by step. That was the important thing. Joey continued his report. "It's being staged by the Galluccis, a bunch of renegades from Brooklyn." He hesitated, then said, "My father doesn't like me saying things like *renegades*, but …" He let the words die away. Grandpa grinned knowingly, then Joey explained the rest.

"The Galluccis have paid a bunch of freelance black hoodlums from Harlem to set your son up. Johnny Gallucci met these guys in prison. They became friends. The word is the Galluccis have nothing against your son. This is a package deal.

"They frame your son for McGlick. McGlick sticks it to someone else. And somehow, a private vendetta of the Galluccis is satisfied. Only Gallucci and his inner circle know the guy they're after."

"And some top cops," Grandpa added.

"We've also located the block where the frame will take place," said Joey, raising his eyebrows. "Hopefully, before nightfall, we'll know which house. My father feels if your son doesn't know which street, he won't overreact. It's best if he falls into the trap. We'll take care of the rest. He must trust us. Tell him to obey the orders of anyone wearing a white carnation. There won't be any niggers wearing carnations on 108th Street." Joey realized he had goofed again by naming the street where the frame would occur. Grandpa knew it too, but neither said anything.

Joey then handed Grandpa a sealed envelope, explaining, "My father wants you to read this then burn it in my presence." Joey shrugged. Grandpa opened the envelope. The instructions were simple: gather some materials and put them into a bundle. Bring the bundle back later. Grandpa then burned the letter, sensing all the while why the don did not want Joey to know what was in it. Joey felt compelled to explain his father's apparent lack of trust in him. "I made a slip at a recent card game, and this is his way of punishing me."

"No," Grandpa said affectionately, "that's his way of teaching you."

"Touché," Joey said, as he opened the car door and left. For the next few minutes, Grandpa sat and thought about what he had been told. While Joey talked, it had all come together. Now, Grandpa carefully reviewed his conclusions, looking for flaws, but found none.

McGlick, Grandpa now felt, was carrying out a heavy contract in the Seventh Division for someone at headquarters. Gallucci had paid this someone enough money to get a certain party in the Seventh Division. Since it was personal and Gallucci couldn't touch it himself, it had to be a cop. Because Joey's sources ruled out Hugh, it had to be Adler. Grandpa's conversation with Hugh regarding the division's attitude toward the Three-nine seemed to confirm that. But why Adler? Who was the power behind the contract at HQ? If he could answer those questions, Grandpa could save both Hugh and Adler, but he couldn't. Frustrated, he started the car and drove home.

Hugh was psyched up. He was having his exiting cup of tea while standing at the front door. He wanted to be especially early today. He would check everything. Once again, Grandpa was meticulous in his instructions, including everything the don wanted Hugh to know without divulging the background of his allies. Grandpa and Bill would serve as Hugh's backup team.

Margaret, naturally apprehensive, kissed and hugged Hugh hard, saying, "Be careful." She wanted to ask him to stay home, to tell Hugh how she needed him in bed beside her, that all this was foolishness, but she said nothing. Hugh smiled, gave everyone the thumbs-up signal, and left.

The bundle had been prepared exactly as the don requested. As Grandpa drove to the 3:00 PM meeting, something gnawed at his subconscious. When he finally retrieved the material, it turned out to be a story his father had told him about an incident in 1866.

The Fenians, a nationwide Irish organization, headquartered at a mansion in Union Square in New York City and dedicated to the freedom of Ireland from England, decided to invade and capture Canada and then swap it for Ireland. It was all so simple. That was what William O'Mahoney, their leader, told Grandpa's father one day in 1866 at a fundraising picnic in the Bronx. After a few beers, O'Mahoney related plans for a simultaneous invasion to be mounted from Buffalo, New York, and St. Albans, Vermont. After a few more beers, Great-Grandpa promised to join the Buffalo contingent.

One pleasant June morning, not long after, six hundred Irishmen from the Buffalo contingent crossed into Canada. There had been eight hundred, but two hundred got so drunk the night before they missed the barges across the river. At the town of Ridgeway, they routed two thousand Canadian troops. They soon discovered that, unfortunately for them, the other strike force never left St. Albans. General George C. Meade, hero of Gettysburg (he didn't drink), under orders from President Johnson, had disarmed and neutralized the St. Albans force. The Buffalo contingent had no choice but to withdraw to the States.

That event and the present situation had one important thing in common: In both cases, there was a lack of communication. That had spelled disaster once and could not be allowed to happen again. For tonight's mission, there had to be some way for the two groups, Irish and Italian, to communicate with one another.

Grandpa wasn't the only one to realize that. Joey handed him a walkie-talkie when they met. Grandpa's face showed his surprise. It shouldn't have come as news to him that the don had extensive experience in battle tactics. Joey read it on his face and smiled.

"We're even," Grandpa said with a grin, as he handed over the wrapped bundle.

✣　✣　✣

Hugh wasn't the only one to arrive early. Captain Stevens was also early. Though a stooge of Yates, Stevens didn't know the entire plan.

He had been told just enough to be able to handle his part. It was an important role for which he expected a generous reward. His first task was to call IAD, the Internal Affairs Division. He informed the inspector in charge that he had received anonymous information that tonight, a newly assigned sergeant named Ryan would sell some junk that he had illegally confiscated while still serving in the Bronx.

The anonymous source, Stevens explained, would call back as soon as the location was pinpointed. Stevens convinced the inspector that Ryan would spot a trail and that IAD should have three or four men waiting in the adjoining precinct. Once the location of the sale was phoned in, Stevens would contact them. Other functions he would perform as the evening progressed would be to make sure Ryan left on foot patrol, ordering Ryan, when he made his 9:30 ring to the TS sergeant, to respond to a phony DOA on 108th Street. [A later investigation would fail to substantiate Grandpa's claim that this order had been given.] Once Ryan was on his way, Stevens would contact the IAD people before personally responding to the scene to search the sergeant for narcotics prior to supervising his arrest. It will be a fun night, thought Stevens while cracking his knuckles.

Don Trataglia's men had pinpointed the location. They were already playing poker in the partially furnished top-floor apartment at 315 East 108th Street, next door to number 317. The five players, all seasoned gangsters, were led by the brutish Bruno Trataglia, the don's oldest son, who had been named after his grandfather. When the signal came, they would move with swift precision over the roof to apartment 5F in number 317 and accomplish their mission.

Oscar Brown, a Harlem-born street fighter, first met Johnny Gallucci in Sing Sing Prison, where both were doing time for manslaughter. They negotiated the treaty that ended the constant racial wars rocking the prison. The world inside prison wasn't so much different from the one outside, Gallucci told Brown. There was just so much territory and business available. This was divided proportionately to the black-white population in the prison. The agreement worked. It became a cash-

and-carry relationship. After being paroled, each man returned to his turf—Brown to Harlem, Gallucci to South Brooklyn. But occasions arose where each would purchase the other's services, knowing that the job would be done—and done well.

Tonight's work presented no problem for Brown. He didn't even have to be there. Bubba and his goons would handle that end. Brown would sit in Small's Bar on Lennox Avenue awaiting their report, then he would depart to a prearranged spot for his cash payment. It had always been that way with Gallucci.

✳ ✳ ✳

The Two-one Precinct station house stood on 129th Street between two abandoned buildings. And of the three, the station house looked the most decrepit. Everything looks normal, thought Hugh, as he got ready for his tour. But the signs were there—and thanks to Grandpa, he recognized them. Hugh had been assigned to foot patrol. And Captain Stevens was there to make sure his feet hit the street. Hugh was relieved. Let's get this over with one way or another, he thought. But win or lose, I'm going down fightin'. He felt good as he dialed the Ryan home. Hugh included in his short conversation the phrase, "Wait for me." It told Grandpa what he already knew: the game was afoot.

✳ ✳ ✳

Bill drove the brown Chevy with Grandpa slouched in the seat next to him. They would follow Hugh at a safe distance, far enough to keep others from spotting them for several hours. Grandpa even considered keeping Hugh away from 108th Street but realized the McGlick-Gallucci-Brown connection would keep pushing this on other fronts until they were convinced they were outgunned, and that could not be done with what Hugh and his friends had available. This would have to be brought to a head, once and for all. And there was no time like the present.

It was difficult for Bill to go along with the arrangement; Grandpa hadn't told him about 108th Street for the same reason he hadn't told Hugh. They were spontaneous individuals, quick, reflexive, emotional men, as he had once been. If they knew too much, Grandpa realized, it would play havoc with their emotions. It would slow their response and hurt their chance for survival. It was simply part of being Irish.

Grandpa, having reached the rhetorical stage of life, calmly puffed on his favorite corncob and prattled on about local, esoteric trivia, much to the annoyance of his keyed-up grandson. It was only when Hugh headed toward 108th Street, after a stop at a local call box, that Grandpa sat up, became silent, and reached for the walkie-talkie.

In McGlick's office, Silent Tony sat playing solitaire, waiting for the coded phone call from Harlem. When it came, he would drive to the 161st Street YMCA, go for a swim, and there give McGlick the word.

Bubba had two men in the street who would follow Ryan into 317 to prevent a possible retreat. As Ryan climbed the stairs to the fifth floor, they would follow. Bubba's other man guarded the roof in case Ryan decided to keep climbing. Once he was trapped in the apartment, where Bubba waited, the rest would be routine. However, if anything went wrong, Brown's final order to Bubba was that if he couldn't frame Ryan, he was to forget it and do nothing more. This was McGlick's doing; he didn't want it to get any nastier or more brutal than it already was.

Bubba now waited, facing the door, a double-barreled sawed-off shotgun on a sling over his shoulder. The bags of heroin were scattered on the table. The hypodermic needle was ready. He would do as Brown ordered but hoped that somehow circumstances would allow him to do this his way.

Hugh slowly approached 317 East 108th Street and stopped alongside the empty police car parked out front. Had this been a legitimate DOA, two cops would have been waiting in the apartment for him to supervise a search of the body and to conduct an inventory of the deceased's property. When Hugh casually but purposely touched the hood of the car, he found it cool and knew this was it.

Grandpa had signaled the Trataglias via walkie-talkie but failed to get a comprehensive response, just static. As Hugh entered the building, Grandpa observed two black winos follow him in. He didn't like it. Panic struck. The damn static. He called and called. There was no response to his feverish pleas for acknowledgment. He felt helpless. By now, it was too late to do anything. He just had to trust in the don. At this point, Bill reminded Grandpa that if they didn't hear anything, their instructions were to cover the rear of the building.

"Then move it," the older man said in an urgent voice. He was glad he had confided somewhat in Bill. They shot off down 108th Street. For the second time in his life, Grandpa admitted he was getting too old for something; the first time he admitted that had been two years earlier, when the subject was touch football.

When he heard the loud knock, Bubba rose, pointing his shotgun at the door. The voice outside shouted, "Police, Two-one Precinct!"

"Come in, Sarge," Bubba yelled, hoping to make Ryan believe a cop was already inside. The door swung open suddenly to reveal a sergeant with a .38-caliber Smith & Wesson in his hand. In automatic response, Bubba pulled both shotgun triggers. At the same time he felt a sting in his side from the fired pistol. Bubba knew he'd been hit but smiled in satisfaction at the bloody, headless sergeant on the floor. Hearing screams in the hall, Bubba retreated to a rear bedroom and down the fire escape. Bruno rushed into the apartment, spotted what lay on the floor, gasped, "Oh, Christ," and raced to the roof.

The three IAD lieutenants were just arriving in front of the building when they heard the shots. The empty police car that had been there minutes earlier was now gone. Upon reaching the fifth floor, the lieutenants were sickened, just as Captain Stevens would be when he arrived a few seconds later. There were sights even hardened cops and gangsters don't take in stride. This was one of them.

Bill and Grandpa heard nothing. But as the minutes passed, they grew extremely edgy. Then, a black Cadillac pulled silently alongside the idling Chevy. Windows were rolled down, and Bruno sadly reported, "We had problems. Drive around to 108th Street. It will all explain itself." Bruno waved farewell, and the Cadillac moved slowly away.

Within minutes, the number 317 flashed through Harlem and the South Bronx faster than the Jersey policy number. On Lennox Avenue, wisdom said this meant trouble. Brown's man had offed a cop. That might lead to police trouble, then a riot. The cops would, of course, move fiercely against Brown's people. He would scream police brutality. Some local politician would support him. Fringe hate groups, looking for an issue around which to ferment trouble, would hit the street with the inevitable outcome.

Tony never received the coded message from Harlem; it came over the division radio instead, frantic, concerned inquiries to the Bronx radio dispatcher about a rumor concerning a sergeant literally blown apart in Harlem. Tony trembled uncontrollably.

He now realized his yearnings for comfort had led him, favor by favor, to this heinous and deadly act. He was scared shitless. It could lead to prison. His remorse was heightened by the fact that this was no ordinary death. Ryan was no derelict or hood, but a fellow cop, who, from all reports, had been an honorable and dedicated officer for nineteen years, a man with a wife and six children.

Later, when Tony reached the pool, where a shaken McGlick waited, he stood zombie-like as McGlick fastened two hands on his shoulders, shook Tony gently, and said it had all been a miscalculation, one of those things that just happened. Tony had squirmed when McGlick, still benumbed himself, handed him the envelope with the money in it. Tony cringed but took it.

Bill and Grandpa, frightened by how Bruno looked and what he said, feared the unthinkable as they drove up and saw the body being carried from the building. They gasped when they spotted the sergeant's chevron on the arm hanging down from the covered stretcher.

Grandpa rushed toward the stretcher crying, "My God, that's my son." Mercifully, several officers prevented him from exposing the corpse and led him back to the Chevy. By now, Grandpa was crumbling, and Bill was in shock. The morgue wagon had already arrived, and the body was carried to it.

At that point, a uniformed sergeant emerged from 315 East 108th Street. It was Hugh Ryan. As Bill and Grandpa raced to embrace him, Hugh spotted the corpse. Stunned at the sight of what could have been him, he felt a weakness in his legs and slumped down onto the stoop of 315.

Captain Stevens, unhinged at the sight of the headless corpse, was completely astonished when he spotted Ryan on the stoop. Unable to speak, Stevens immediately left for the station house to make some fast calls and to squelch street rumors about the death of a police sergeant.

Only later did Hugh tell Grandpa and Bill how he entered 317 and was taken over the roof into 315 by Trataglia's men, after they jacked the hoods who had followed Hugh and tied up Bubba's guard on the roof. To everyone else, Hugh simply said, "I made a mistake and went into the wrong building."

All this did not wipe away the mess, which Bruno had said was self-explanatory. The old, untraceable uniform, with laundry marks and police numbers removed, the bundle that Grandpa had provided, had led to the death of the trusted Trataglia lieutenant. It was the cause of the sadness Bruno meant to convey. What had been planned as a quiet operation on both sides had now ended in disaster. But at least Hugh was alive and safe for yet another day.

An investigation was started immediately and lasted all night. Ryan stuck to his story about having gone into the wrong building to check on the DOA. Captain Stevens and the TS sergeant denied having sent him anywhere. The whole mess smelled so badly that even the IAD wanted nothing to do with it. As a result of a decision in headquarters, Ryan received only an oral warning for being off post. The dead man was classified as a police impostor, killed while trying to rip-off a black drug factory.

Grandpa was disappointed by the outcome. His hope that the plot against Hugh would be irreparably exposed wasn't realized. Fast footwork expertly downgraded the incident, and the night's activities drew no media attention. Once again, the curtain of secrecy was carefully and skillfully drawn over the players by the distraught and shaken Stevens, after some clever advice and help from higher up.

THE POLICE COMMISSIONER was pleased with the way Yates had handled the Harlem situation. Even the unseasoned O'Grady recognized how close they had come to a major catastrophe. Yates had ordered Stevens to immediately disseminate, by radio, a phony drug rip-off story to all on-duty cops and to all outgoing platoons. It was the reaction of the ordinary cop on the beat that had Yates worried. He knew how difficult they were to control when one of their own had been murdered. Every punk, hood, and, unfortunately, even some innocent citizens would fall prey to overzealous officers responding to just such a situation. Like McGlick, Yates too had been relieved that a disguised Mafia hood, not Ryan, had been killed. Yates had pushed for this type of frame and realized how close to a riot things had come. That event would have led to his ouster by an irate mayor before his Gallucci retirement money came through. Just how close Yates had come to losing his job was brought home when Bruce Koppel, the mayoral aide responsible for financing the mayor's reelection campaign, charged into his office.

The mayor, a basically honest man, had inherited Koppel and retained him because of his legendary ability to raise funds. The mayor had his suspicions about the man, but being a pragmatic politician, he kept Koppel. Without strong financing, both the mayor's reelection campaign and his planned gubernatorial challenge two years hence would fail. Of course, if even a hint of Koppel's wrongdoing hit the papers, radio, or TV, the mayor would indignantly fire him. Koppel understood this; he had worked under that implicit threat for the last two mayors. Today, he was visiting Yates, his corruption pipeline in the police department.

"What the hell is wrong with you?" Koppel scolded. "McGlick was behind that fiasco in Harlem, wasn't he?" To protect himself, Yates let all the blame fall on McGlick and nodded yes.

Yates said, "Relax, Bruce, everything is under control."

Koppel didn't buy it. "Under control?" he spit in contempt. "We risk a near race riot, an incipient mob war. You call that under control? Either one of those things could devastate the mayor politically. Don't you read the papers? That Republican SOB from Staten Island who wants the mayor's job has already made crime the major issue in the upcoming election." Koppel shook his head in disgust. "How could you give McGlick the okay on this?"

Yates was glad McGlick was getting most of the blame but wanted to smooth things over for both of them. "Look, the Adler case is wrapped up. There was no riot, and I'll make sure the families don't war on one another. Relax."

Koppel, still irritated, shot back, "Well, here's something to make you relax. One more foul-up, and you're out." He stomped toward the door, pulled it open, and without looking back, said, "By the way, last night will cost you five thousand." He left without waiting for an answer.

A shaken Yates tried to forget the money and turned his attention to the more pressing problem of trying to prevent a war between the families. Wiping his brow, he suddenly realized that his little pond had turned into a raging, storming ocean, and in that ocean, he would sink or swim.

To handle sensitive matters between the mob and the police, there existed a group known as the Triumvirate, a deputy inspector and two captains. It was not a group shown on any organizational chart as their function did not welcome public awareness. Basically, the unit conciliated territorial differences between the five families. After all, business was business and gang wars interrupted monthly payoffs, not to mention all the bad publicity, which put pressure on the mayor and the police to control these gangsters. It was this business end of things between the mob and the police which had doomed Adler and made him a marked man. Years before, he had made an honest mistake in Brooklyn for which he would now pay.

His mind made up after only a few minutes of thought, Yates buzzed his secretary on the intercom. "Call Deputy Inspector Green, Captain Donnelly, and Captain Zelnick. Invite them to a one o'clock lunch at Patsy's on Broome Street." Yates was still apprehensive. He thought for one second, hit the buzzer again, and said, "Get me McGlick on the line."

✳ ✳ ✳

By the sheer brilliance of his tactics, Don Trataglia led his family to dominance in the 1947 war between the families. During the past few years, his position had weakened somewhat. However, Trataglia placed this in perspective. He believed the council should be a forum of equals. So, as others slowly increased their power over various enterprises, Trataglia openly encouraged them at council meetings. He wanted it understood he was not doing this out of weakness, but from the realization that true harmony, and increased profits, could best be obtained from equalized power and cooperation between partners. Following that path, Trataglia was in the process of arranging a countrywide family conclave at Apalachin, New York, to address the national and international aspects of their business. It was time to incorporate, he liked to say.

To resolve the difficulties created by the Harlem incident, Trataglia had called today's council meeting. He planned to complain to the Galluccis about their using a group of trigger-happy, black hoodlums for what should have been a nonviolent and simple assignment. He had, after all, lost a valuable and trusted lieutenant in this affair. He would ask the council for a ruling on the propriety of the Galluccis operating in his territory, even if on a personal matter, without first getting permission.

The don heard two honks of a car horn. It meant his men were waiting to take him into the city. He looked out a side window. His wife, Nina, a charming, plump Neapolitan, was pruning her azalea bush. The don smiled. If only life was truly that simple and beautiful, he thought. Why are things so complicated? He couldn't answer that question. He didn't believe anyone could.

❈ ❈ ❈

The Ryan house was silent. The damn phone had everyone on edge—a Pavlovian response. Ring—trouble. Ring—trouble. When it rang this time, Hugh grabbed the two-headed plastic and electronic serpent.

"Yeah," he said harshly into the mouthpiece.

"Sarge?" a voice on the other end asked.

"Yeah," Hugh said once more, his voice rising in anticipation.

"This is roll call. Your squad has been changed. Instead of coming in at 4:00 PM, report in at midnight."

Another "yeah" came from Hugh.

Grandpa wasn't surprised at this latest development. "There are probably some high-level meetings going on," he said. "No doubt, they're trying to decide on their next move. Stevens doesn't want anything unauthorized happening. That's a good sign."

Hugh could not accept Grandpa's optimism. "Let's stop this Pollyanna crap," Hugh demanded in a quivering voice. "They tried to kill me last night; that's what's real. You were there. So they changed my squad. That's a good sign? Stop it, Pa, please!"

Grandpa put an arm around his son. "Believe me, Hugh, the worst is over. You must believe that. It's the only way to survive."

Hugh understood. He wanted to believe, but, for now, his spirit had been shattered.

❈ ❈ ❈

McGlick stared out his office window at the street below. He was watching two young blacks strip a vouchered car opposite the station house. He alerted the desk sergeant.

When he put the phone down, he began to pace the floor again thinking about the foul-up on 108th Street. Yates had called and ordered McGlick not to say anything to anyone about the Ryan matter, as if McGlick was thinking of doing otherwise.

Had Ryan been killed, thought McGlick, what a disaster that would have been. Luckily, it didn't happen. He hadn't even wanted this kind of frame, but Yates insisted. It irked him that the operation wasn't carried out in the Bronx. It would have been done right up here, he thought.

McGlick hated relying on others. He wanted to control his own destiny. Even Tony was beginning to worry him.

What bothered McGlick still more was that Yates threatened him, under threat of demotion to captain, not to move directly against Hugh Ryan. And why should Yates care about Ryan? Ryan was no threat to him. Adler was on his way out. Yates had what he wanted. But Ryan was still a dagger in McGlick's heart. Dammit! He had to go. Now that things were rolling, now that the iron was hot, now was the time to strike and get results.

Stalking the office, McGlick suddenly grinned. Yates hadn't said anything about not touching the old buzzard or the young, arrogant kid at the academy. That could be another way of putting pressure on Ryan to quit while the quitting was good.

McGlick sat down at his desk and began opening that morning's mail. As he slit open the third envelope, he froze. It contained a Photostat of a news clipping showing the execution of Lieutenant Charles Becker for the Rosenthal murder. The frenzy, when it came this time, would have the entire division office running for cover. It came maybe one day too late, but Grandpa had made his point.

✳ ✳ ✳

It could have been a board meeting of five Chase Manhattan Bank officers in that plush midtown conference room with the huge oaken table, deep red leather chairs, and the open bar. But it wasn't. New York's five crime czars were meeting to straighten out one of their own.

Don Trataglia called the meeting to order and quickly outlined the Harlem incident with all its ramifications. He explained his own personal interest in seeing that Ryan wasn't harmed or framed by anyone on the council. There followed a lengthy discussion, during which the council ruled that the Galluccis had overstepped their authority regardless of the nature of their vendetta and that prior consultation and approval would be required in any future territorial intrusions. Gallucci then apologized for the death in the Trataglia family and offered generous financial assistance to the dead man's wife and children.

Trataglia accepted the offer but insisted that Gallucci reveal the nature of his vendetta. Reluctantly, for he knew the council's policy on cop killing, which had been strengthened after the McCloskey affair, Gallucci revealed that Adler was the marked man.

Gallucci knew it was a calculated risk. The council had the power to void his aspirations. But with the powerful Trataglia's personal interest, the mistake in Harlem, and his own unorthodox approach to Adler's demise, he knew he had to tell all and resign himself to the decision of the tribunal.

"Well," he began, "this goes back a number of years to when Marvin Adler was still a lieutenant. He had been one for a long time. He finally made the captains list. So they sent him to South Brooklyn as boss of the local plainclothes men. From what I'm told, he did what every other lieutenant on the captains list in a similar assignment does; he did nothing. Adler stayed in his office, hoped for an early promotion, avoided his men, and openly displayed a tape recorder on his desk which, he let it be known, was used to record all conversations, both in person and on the phone.

"Then, one afternoon, he received an anonymous call informing him that a local bookie was moving that day's work. The sheets with that day's gambling action, who bet how much on what, were being taken to another location.

"Suspecting a setup, he led the raid himself, confiscating $187,000 and several days' sheets. The money meant shit, but without sheets, as you know, false claims have to be paid. Some cops will sell the sheets back or at least check them to verify large bets."

Gallucci began to waver, his voice cracking as he said, "So it was that Don Carlo, over there, called Adler about the sheets." He stopped to point at Don Carlo. The other man showed no surprise, continuing to stare at the frescos on the ceiling. Gallucci took a sip of his Bacardi before going on, a bit less tension in his voice now.

"Adler refused to sell the sheets back, so Don Carlo asked him to check out a $500 bet made by a young kid. That poor kid was my little brother."

Don Carlo now stared in confusion at Gallucci. "You don't even remember," Gallucci said, obviously stunned by the lack of recognition.

Annoyed at the emotional outburst, Trataglia commanded, "Just tell the story."

Gallucci gulped down the remainder of his drink and went on. "Adler put down the phone. I later heard he commented about the arrogance of those guinea hoods. A few minutes later, he picked up the line and said, 'No good.' Don Carlo misinterpreted that to mean the bet was phony." Once again, Gallucci paused to stare at Don Carlo, but Trataglia motioned him to continue.

"The next day, my kid brother, Sally, was found floating in the river near the Brooklyn Navy Yard, his tongue cut out with a pair of shears."

Don Carlo rubbed his creased forehead with the knuckle of his right thumb, his head tilted down, his eyes closed. Gallucci watched then screamed, "It was in his wallet. You remember, Don. You put Sally's tongue in his wallet!"

Don Carlo opened his eyes, looked unblinkingly at Gallucci, and said, "Yes, I remember, I remember." The acknowledgment seemed to calm the ranting Gallucci. To murder was business, but to forget it was disrespectful. More than anything, Gallucci wanted respect. He went on.

"Adler's promotion came on the day me and my brothers found out the truth. Sally had made the $500 bet. From that day on, scumbag Adler was a marked man." He looked around for visible support. There was none, so he continued. "At the time, Yates was a deputy chief in Brooklyn. Because of Adler's lack of respect, my boss, I was just a soldier then, refused to make any payments to Yates for months. Since we were the biggest bank in the borough, that hurt him in the pocket.

"I know the problems associated with cop killings, so I waited patiently for years to make my move. Then I got worried as Adler's career moved upward. When Yates made chief inspector, I saw my chance. Koppel, the mayor's man, was contacted and agreed, at a price, to be a go-between. Yates's job was to undermine and retire Adler. Neither Koppel nor Yates is aware I plan to kill Adler. Yates has forced loads of top brass out of their jobs for the pleasure of it. He was delighted to get paid to eliminate another guy, especially Adler." Gallucci looked around the table.

"To my knowledge, the council has no rules about killing ex-cops. Just to be on the safe side, I intend to wait one year after Adler is out before I make my move." Gallucci rested his case.

The council was annoyed that this had not been brought to their attention earlier. True, it was personal, but it also affected business. Killing a cop or ex-cop was always business of the most serious kind. Trataglia wasn't completely sympathetic to Gallucci's plan for revenge but wanted to hear from the others.

One don sided with Gallucci. He argued that this affair was a matter of family honor to the increasingly powerful Galluccis. A lengthy, vigorous, and peaceful debate followed. Don Carlo, head of the Corlese family, pointed out that everyone there had had fathers, brothers, and sons killed in the business—killed by others in that very room. But revenge had to be put aside, as in the past, or business would be hurt. Don Vincini from Staten Island agreed with Don Carlo. That made it two against two. The deciding vote rested with Trataglia.

His decision was swift. "All future actions for or against Adler or Ryan by this council will immediately cease. As punishment for Adler, the agreed upon fee will be paid to force him out, but that's where it ends. Adler is not to be killed, but that Harlem bunch of Brown's is to be severely punished." They all knew that this was tantamount to a death sentence.

"The consigliere from each family will meet the police Triumvirate to ensure that the council's decrees are adhered to without exception. The police Triumvirate will be informed that in the future, neither we nor the police will accept contracts that interfere with the internal discipline or the political structure of the other's organization."

Trataglia knew this wouldn't help Ryan, but all leaders soon find that organizational goals must take precedence over personal feelings. It wasn't the first unpleasant decision he had made—it wouldn't be the last. At the same time, he sincerely believed he had repaid his family debt and that Grandpa Ryan would agree. The don now declared the matter closed. All eyes turned to the usually hot-headed Gallucci. Surprisingly, he agreed, though he wished it could have been otherwise. One by one, the other dons rose and went to hug Gallucci, recognizing he had surrendered his individuality for the sake of unity. No longer would he be considered a renegade. The council had never been stronger.

✳   ✳   ✳

Uncle Fred and Aunt Grace were matched against Hugh and Margaret in a spirited game of pinochle. Margaret led a queen of trump to Grace and then winced when a glance at Hugh revealed his annoyance. Grace played a king. Hugh, sitting with an ace, a ten, and a jack of spades, which was trump for this deal, was required by the rules to play a higher trump if he had one. Not knowing where the other ace of spades lay, Hugh was forced to play his ace and took the trick. Unfortunately, when Grace got the lead back, she played her ace, then her ten of trump captured Hugh's ten which cost the game. Margaret, Grace, and Fred expected Hugh's usual lecture, but he had mellowed since the McGlick incident and instead just nodded and grinned.

The crisis had calmed Hugh, though the strain was evident on his thinning face. It had, however, made the weekend card games more pleasurable. No one had enjoyed Hugh's competitive outbursts.

Not only had he improved in this respect, but Hugh was also a better husband and father now. Little family matters had become more important. The sulking child received greater encouragement; the tired wife was relieved of some minor drudgery or given a back rub. The family had already decided that once the troubles were resolved, Hugh should retire. He had agreed.

After the game, Hugh got his things and left for work with some degree of optimism. Grandpa, who took Hugh's place in the game, convinced him that tomorrow would hold some good news.

HIRSCHEL HAD PUT Raoul to bed shortly after midnight, the last night this would be required. Tomorrow night, he would make the headline arrest with all the attendant glory.

Earlier, a snappily dressed Guzman had visited a number of 138th Street bars then staggered back to his apartment. If Raoul suspected a tail, he certainly didn't show it.

At 4:00 AM, Hirschel, aware that Guzman's normal period of attack had passed, headed for his Manhattan loft to catch a few hours sleep. Though the extra money from this job would finance a trip to the Caribbean with his latest girlfriend and add some stereo components to the sophisticated system at his loft, he was relieved this thing was coming to an end. Over the past days, he had done a complete background check on Guzman. The progressive viciousness associated with the series of rapes meant but one thing to the experienced detective: If Guzman were allowed to strike again, it could lead to a grisly homicide.

✳   ✳   ✳

Hugh was back on TS tonight. After last night's fiasco, Stevens had obviously received new orders. The precinct was buzzing with theories and rumors as to the meaning of the headless sergeant. A cop, passing through the muster room, yelled out to Hugh, "Hey, Sarge, have a headache tonight!" Hugh heard the laughter from the sitting room and smiled. Their kidding was a sign of acceptance into the club; most cops there had a higher-ranking enemy in the department. This was a dumping ground, like the Forty-first Precinct in the Bronx, the Seventy-fifth in Brooklyn, and the Ninth, also in Manhattan. They were places of punishment and harassment—the foreign legion garrisons of the police department. Ryan thought he could take it for his final year, but he felt jittery tonight, wondering what new crap was being planned for him.

Before yesterday, thought Hugh, my only worries were for my job and my pension. Now, my ass is on the line too. Hugh had carried the burden with dignity, realizing hysterics and complaining achieved little. He knew his enemies—and they weren't the cops of the Two-one.

Bruno Trataglia, his father's consigliere, was always amused by the locations the police chose for these secret late-night meetings. Tonight, it was a dilapidated garage south of Fort Lee, New Jersey. The five families could safely meet in a richly furnished midtown office without fear, but the Triumvirate distrusted everything associated with wealth. In corrupt circles, it was a cliché that the greediest cops drove the oldest cars, the kind even honest cops wouldn't touch. Crooked cops, Bruno knew, took great pains to disguise their hidden wealth. But as Don Trataglia had taught his son, it was impossible to hide dishonesty from a discerning observer. Sometimes Bruno and his father would play a little game trying to decide if a new cop on the beat near their Manhattan import business was honest. After a short, friendly talk with the cop, touching only on everyday matters, the don would pick correctly. Bruno always lost when betting against his father.

Don Trataglia had immediately realized Hugh was an honest cop. Grandpa had casually mentioned how Bill dropped out of CCNY to join the army before going into the police force. An Irish Catholic cop from the Bronx would never send his son to CCNY in Manhattan if he could afford schools such as Fordham and Iona. The Trataglias often laughed at how many Irish lawyers, engineers, bankers, and priests they had put through college.

Once over the George Washington Bridge, Bruno's bodyguard headed their car south past Palisades Amusement Park then turned east toward the Hudson. They reached their destination, parked, and got out.

Bruno went downhill toward a row of leaning garages but paused a moment, startled by the angular steel and yellow-lighted beauty of Manhattan, which loomed across the silver-ribboned waters of the Hudson. He quickly pushed this from his mind and went on. More practical matters tugged at his attention.

As soon as Bruno entered the garage, where the other four consiglieri had arrived shortly after the Triumvirate and two black policy bankers, Captain Zelnick handed him a wooden milk crate to sit on. Bruno took it with a look of amusement, added it to the circle of crates that had been formed, and sat down.

Deputy Inspector Green then quickly expressed Yates's two major concerns: a possible Harlem riot precipitated by some mob retribution against Brown, and his fear that the 108th Street incident might lead to a five-borough gang war. Yates had told Green of his shock at how one pebble, tossed into a small pond occupied by himself, McGlick, Stevens, Ryan, and a few other players, had touched such distant shores and sent shock waves into other, larger ponds, creating a tidal wave that threatened to engulf all of them. It brought to mind a story Green had read, years earlier, about how Austro-Hungary had planned a limited attack against the small nation of Serbia. This was all it was intended to be, a limited punishment strike. Instead, a minor miscalculation led to World War I.

Bruno now rose and said, "I am authorized to speak for the council." As he did so, his eyes scanned the circle of milk boxes. "Be assured, there will be no war. However, a retaliatory strike must be sanctioned against Brown and Bubba, his main lieutenant." Bruno sat back down.

"Short and sweet once again, huh, Bruno?" Inspector Green said, annoyed at Bruno's authoritative approach. "We're here to discuss these problems, not to take orders from the council," Green added. Bruno was impassive.

Green turned to the black bankers. "How do you feel about getting Brown?"

One of the bankers, a huge man with two gold front teeth, appropriately nicknamed Golden Spike, said, "We'd like to kill those motherfuckers, too. They've hit our banks a number of times, but I don't think the mob should make this hit." He paused for some reaction.

Bruno pulled on his ear and asked, "Well, how the hell should it be done?"

"Let's make it a setup with the cops handling it," Spike replied. "I'll leak word of a big cash drop. They'll bite."

Green agreed, saying, "Yates will buy it."

Bruno continued pulling at his right ear and counted the nods of the other consiglieri. He reluctantly agreed. A few more minor matters were straightened out.

After the black policy bankers left, Bruno told Yates's men about the new mutual nonintervention proposal. He expected some flack. To his surprise, the Triumvirate quickly agreed to it. "Yates had already talked about the need for such a policy," said Green. It had been a conciliatory meeting. Both sides suspected that an historic agreement had been reached. Eventually, when Don Trataglia called a national council business meeting at Apalachin, New York, he hoped to have his nonintervention proposal adopted as a national policy. Neither side realized it at the time, but this would be the last meeting between the Triumvirate and the five families. The foul-up at Apalachin would ensure that. With all the national mob leaders trapped by New York State Troopers and the FBI inside an Apalachin farmhouse, mutual tolerance was dealt a fatal blow. Gallucci made an attempt to escape in his underwear but was roughly tackled by a young trooper. However, Don Trataglia and Don Carlo did manage to make it safely through the woods to freedom. But an era had ended—institutionalized cooperation at the top levels between the police and the mob was dead.

Many cops in the Three-nine Precinct were happy when Ryan was transferred out. Though fair, he was tough. He expected the men under him to make their rings on time, to be on post for their 2:00 AM and 6:00 AM "sees" on the late tour, and to do other things that ensured they were, at the very least, providing adequate coverage on their posts.

With Ryan gone, his squads fell under the direction of Sergeant Dan Crenshaw, who was in his usual inebriated condition tonight. A good night's sleep was guaranteed for everyone. No rings or "sees" would take place this night. Even the special cops assigned to search for the rapist retired to various coops after the rapist's expected striking hours had come and passed.

Every precinct, however, had a few diehards who patrolled all night regardless of who was over them. They were known as O'Learys, named after a legendary cop, who did straight eights for over thirty years under all weather conditions. Dutch Van Buren was an O'Leary. So tonight, while others rested after the bars closed, Dutch moved slowly from one store doorway to the next, first checking the door then standing in the shallow, shadowed entrance for a short time checking 138th Street in both directions before moving on.

It had never happened to Raoul before, after getting a drunk on, but inexplicably, the urge came over him around 4:00 AM. Looking into the street below, the still and victimless avenue galled him. Then he remembered the comely Puerto Rican girl he had followed a week ago. He had been steered off by another voice in her apartment. He couldn't believe it, but he hoped that someone else would be there again. The violation would be greater and the thrill heightened. Dressing rapidly, he made sure he had his linen napkin properly secreted, his new gravity knife and apartment key on him, and nothing more.

As the rapist emerged from 475, Van Buren spotted him immediately. The nattily dressed Guzman strode purposefully east on 138th Street, crossed to Van Buren's side, and headed south on Cypress Avenue toward St. Mary's Park. It was not an unusual event in this section of the city, some John returning home to the wife and kids after a little pleasure, but Dutch noted it was 4:15 AM. The scarcity of pedestrians on the street would cause him to remember this particular moment, especially in light of the events which followed.

Raoul made a left on 141st Street, a right on Crimmins to Oak Street, a short block just south of the park, then climbed an eight-foot, wire-mesh fence, putting him at the rear of the Oak Street tenements. Within seconds, he was climbing a fire escape to the targeted apartment. The only air conditioners in the South Bronx are open windows, and on this hot, humid August night, the greatest possible cross-ventilation was desirable.

Flipping open the seven-inch gravity knife, Raoul entered through the open kitchen window and tiptoed through the apartment in search of a victim. The symbol of his dominance was growing already, its blood pulsating wildly as he anticipated the debauchery ahead. Staring into one bedroom, he saw two sleeping female children. He knew what he would do if he didn't find an older female. Fortunately for the children, Raoul found the object of his desire sleeping next to her husband in an adjoining room. Under ordinary circumstances, Raoul was an extremely powerful man, an athlete of considerable ability in his youth, but during these excursions, his strength and ability, not to mention his sexual drive, became superhuman, as his previous victims had embarrassingly reported.

Holding the linen napkin to his face with his left hand, he put the knife to the young woman's throat and harshly said, "Wake up, wake up." As she partially woke and began to sit up, she felt the sharp knife at her throat and gasped, "Oh, my God," in shock.

The outcry, though softened by the increased pressure of the knife, caused her husband to jump up from a lying position on the bed to his knees. His wife's throat had already been slightly cut and a thin trickle of blood ran down onto her thin nightgown.

"Make one move and your wife's dead," Raoul calmly told the trembling man. "Turn over and lie on your stomach with your hands straight out." The terrified and twitching husband complied, well aware he was dealing with a maniac.

Raoul ripped off the see-through gown and began fondling the woman's tense body. "Lay down on your husband, face down," he ordered. Reluctantly, sobbing, she did so.

Raoul caressed her small breasts with his knife, as he began his buggery. "How do you like it, bitch?" he asked angrily. She didn't answer. He sliced at her breast with the knife. Blood gushed out. "I like, I like," the terrified woman cried out. Raoul thrust rapidly and ejaculated. "More, bitch?" he shouted. Again she didn't answer. This time he moved the knife like a scythe across her husband's side. He screamed in pain. "More, more!" the frightened woman screamed. Raoul began to thrust rapidly once again. The process was repeated three more times. Each time, the wound inflicted went deeper.

Then he ordered. "Turn over." The woman quickly complied. Raoul placed the linen napkin over her face. "You're a whore!" he screamed as he began to chop at the man and wife with his blade. The woman pleaded, "*No mas, no mas, por favor,*" as her tears saturated the linen napkin, which now outlined her pretty face. Her sobbing and pleading only resulted in greater abuse.

The frantic husband decided that death was better than allowing this madman to continue torturing his wife. He pushed up and sideways, unseating the pile-driving Raoul, rolled over, and grabbed for the knife. Raoul was faster and, in one thrust, shoved the blade hard into the husband's chest. The man, gasping for air, shivered momentarily and fell back onto the bed, dead. The nude woman, dripping blood, ran for the door.

Raoul pushed the body onto the floor. Two giant leaps and he caught the fleeing woman by the hair. His rage was now unlimited. Her husband could no longer witness the devastation. After sodomizing the woman several times, he Jack-the-Rippered her, leaving her screaming, trying to control the bleeding with the linen napkin. The two young girls saw their mother and wailed hysterically.

This had been his greatest night, he thought, as he climbed out the window and started down the fire escape. He stopped when he saw the building superintendent coming up the fire escape, shotgun in hand. The super, a young Puerto Rican, aroused by the screams, was well aware of the series of rapes in the community and had prepared himself for this eventuality.

Raoul turned and raced up toward the roof, figuring he could jump to the roof of an adjoining building and escape. The super fired. He hit the railing to Raoul's left. The second shot caught Raoul slightly on the right shoulder. Once on the roof, Raoul saw his predicament; there was at least a twenty-foot gap between buildings, the roof door was locked, and that shotgun was coming closer every second.

As the super reached the roof, Raoul made a quick decision. He took a running leap and flew through the air, disappearing into the darkness. The super rapidly fired two more shots and ran to the roof's edge. He shook his head in disbelief. Raoul had safely jumped the chasm.

When the police arrived, somewhat more slowly than usual, their search for the killer turned up nothing. The wife was taken by radio car to the hospital. She survived several hours of surgery and the removal of her reproductive system.

Captain Adler responded to the scene from his home in the hope that perhaps this time, the "Linen Rapist," as the *Bronx Home News* had dubbed him, had made some mistake that would trip him up. Every off-duty detective working on the case was called at home and directed to report immediately to the precinct.

The rapist had killed and would kill again once the blood lust returned. Al Hirschel and Gordon Davis were two of those returned to duty.

A tear came to Adler's eyes when he saw the two young girls of the victims. A policewoman was attempting to calm them down. Adler thought of his own two little girls and how they had cried after the divorce. He too had tried to calm them but couldn't. His wife, Clara, had gotten custody and taken them to California. Some surfer had gotten into her pants and ruined their lives—Well, at least mine, he thought. That seemed so long ago. He had remarried; the kids visited each summer, but somehow, it was never the same.

The screams of a neighborhood woman brought him back to the present. "Why you no catch him?" she yelled at Adler. It's a good question, he thought. Why can't we catch this bastard? Adler was having self-doubts. Maybe McGlick is right. Maybe I'm doing a lousy job. Shit. We should have gotten this guy. I can't understand it. Shit. I'm finished now anyway. Adler realized that this was the lowest point in his life since the divorce.

Though he had taken some pellets in the shoulder, Raoul safely returned to his apartment. He could take care of the wound himself; the last thing he would do was go to a hospital.

Detectives were already checking the hospitals. The super claimed he had hit the rapist at least once. A canvass of buildings in the area was begun. A temporary HQ was set up at the scene. Everyone present was burdened with the pressure of finding the killer. Every possibility had to be explored, documented, correlated, and analyzed. The man had to be stopped.

Davis had never seen Hirschel take a homicide so hard. "The dirty bastard, the dirty bastard," Hirschel kept repeating. Davis figured that the seamy side of police work had finally gotten to Hirschel. He would not be the first, nor would he be the last man to collapse under the burden, thought Davis.

Hirschel knew he had blown it; the filthy psycho had outsmarted him. In his heart, he wept for the poor husband who had defended his wife to the death; he wept for the brutalized, dehumanized woman. Most of all, he wept for himself, his culpability, his avarice, his folly. Hirschel was slipping over the edge. He was physically sick. His stomach ached. His head twirled. His chest heaved. "You stupid motherfucker," he told himself over and over. It had seemed such an easy score. Now he was as much a murderer as Raoul. He knew Raoul's capabilities. How could he have been so fuckin' stupid? Hadn't he figured out the rapist's mental condition. He felt the need to talk, to discuss this massacre he had allowed to happen. Hirschel phoned Silent Tony.

It was 5:00 AM when the phone rang in Tony's bedroom. Though aghast at the news, Tony quickly silenced Hirschel, warning him about using the phone for sensitive communications. "Pull yourself together, man," Tony pleaded. "I'll meet you at 8:00 AM at the usual place. Things will work out. Relax, okay?" After a long pause, Hirschel agreed. For the next three hours, Hirschel would hold in his feelings and continue to move about in a no-exit hell.

The hospitalized woman's description of her attacker reminded Gordon Davis of the derelict he had frisked some days earlier outside the church. He had a hunch. He would have mentioned it to his partner, but Hirschel now appeared to be in a catatonic state as he sat at his desk and stared out the second-floor window at the Manhattan skyline to the south.

Locating the knife in his locker, Davis flipped it open and closely examined the blade as he returned with it to the squad office. There were two ways to close a gravity knife, with the palm of the hand or with the thumb and forefinger. Davis was lucky. The guy had used his fingers.

Using a furot ostrich feather and dark powder, he dusted the blade and uncovered a thumbprint. He dusted the other side and uncovered a second print. Utilizing a special tape, Davis lifted the prints from the metal and placed the adhesive onto a white card. The two distinct prints would be forwarded to the latent print section of the Bureau of Criminal Identification (BCI) for comparison with partial prints found at the scene of the present homicide and earlier rapes.

The police didn't have the practical capability to check the millions of prints on file to determine to whom these prints belonged, but they were useful if the detectives had a suspect. They could prove a man innocent or guilty. In most cases, partial prints were useless, never being connected to any criminal. Yet, some sensational cases had been solved in just this manner.

McDarby's was closed when Hirschel arrived at a quarter to eight. Frank, the daytime bartender, recognized the steady customer and unlocked the door to let him in. Hirschel quickly explained that he had an early meeting. As a retired cop, Frank understood the nature of such meetings and accommodated the visibly troubled Hirschel by leading him into the boss's office. When Tony arrived, a few minutes later, Frank led him into the office and left behind a bottle of Dewars Scotch and two glasses on the desk, sensing both men could use it. They did.

Between gulps of whiskey, Hirschel explained his failure. "I should have brought in help," he said. "Goddamn it, I needed help!"

"You sure did," said Tony, without sarcasm. Although Tony was irritated with Hirschel, he wasn't looking backward. Decisions had to be made.

"I had him mapped out perfect," moaned Hirschel. "I could tell ya where he was at any minute."

Tony resisted the temptation to reply. He was worried. It was obvious that Hirschel was in an unstable mental state.

"You need some time, Al," he said. "Go sick or take your vacation."

"Poor guy," said Hirschel, lowering his head.

Tony knew that unless Hirschel was taken off center stage, he might blow the entire deal and bring down Tony, for sure, and possibly others as well. It took an hour for Tony to persuade Hirschel to take an emergency vacation. He assured the detective that an additional two grand would be provided to ease his mental anguish. Only after Hirschel left did Tony concentrate on his own next move—on his own survival.

The Two-one had been quiet tonight. Hugh, working the switchboard again, heard of the rape-homicide in the Three-nine. It disturbed him. With all the manpower on that case an arrest should already have been made. The longer a criminal eluded a police dragnet the more a whispered theory surfaced that perhaps it was a cop doing these things. That was Hugh's thought as he signed off TS for the day after the tour sergeant signed in then started up to the third-floor locker room.

He felt the sudden, constrictive viselike pain in his chest, the lightning sharp pain down his left arm, and a sudden weakness. He collapsed on the second-floor landing, gasping for air, crying out weakly for help. A young detective, Phil Romano, heard the cry and rushed to Hugh's side.

Having been a medic during the Korean War, Phil recognized the symptoms and knew Ryan's chances of survival were only 15 percent unless he got to a hospital fast; ventricular fibrillation had to be prevented. Hugh was scared. He was positive he would die and became nauseous, vomiting on the stairs. An old-time patrolman, who had suffered from angina pectoris for years, slipped one of his nitroglycerin pills under Ryan's tongue; it didn't help. Acting under Romano's orders, three officers picked Hugh up and carried him out to a waiting radio car. Romano went along, trying to allay Hugh's fear.

They raced toward Harlem Hospital, which was probably the best place in the city to be taken if you'd been shot or stabbed. Practice makes perfect, and at Harlem Hospital, they got plenty of it. For heart attack cases, Romano preferred Columbia Presbyterian, but Harlem was closer and time was of the essence. Ryan's heartbeat fluctuated from rapid to weak. He had minutes, perhaps only seconds left. Romano began mouth-to-mouth resuscitation and screamed to the driver, "Goddamn it, hurry! He can't last much longer!"

When they carried him into the emergency ward, Ryan was unconscious. His shirt was ripped off by a black doctor and a defibrillator was placed on his chest. Several shocks were applied. Hugh was lucky; he pulled through.

Margaret was rushed, by police car, to the hospital. She stayed there for the rest of the day, holding Hugh's hand, speaking softly to him, trying to reduce his anxiety, his fear of death. Grandpa, Bill, Rick, and Kevin came too, but after a short stay, they left at Margaret's urging to take care of the little ones and family business. This was her duty alone. That was the Irish way.

Tony, a survivor for all seasons, was upset by the news of Ryan's second close call with death. He had been on the force over twenty years and in that time, had cleverly used the system, had found its flaws and taken the financial rewards. But for the first time in his career, he was frightened. It was his special capacity for survival that made him feel this way.

Hirschel was cracking. Ryan had been pushed too far. The rapist had struck again. McGlick was a big question mark. The chief inspector was furious and scared. The Galluccis were upset, and more importantly, he wasn't sure what the Trataglias would do now that Ryan faced possible death in Harlem Hospital. Tony feared the Trataglias. If crossed, they were more ruthless than the Galluccis. The Galluccis could be bought off, even on personal family matters. It was a matter of record. Don Trataglia, destined to be the last of the godfathers, would not be turned aside. His decisions were irrevocable. Before Tony made a final decision, he would discuss it with McGlick.

A pale McGlick welcomed a wary Tony into his office. "I've prepared the transfer papers on Adler," he announced in a low, even voice. "The fact that the rapist struck again and murdered this time finishes Adler. I guess Yates has what he wants." Tony nodded. "A nasty business, that rape-murder," McGlick added. Tony nodded again without saying anything.

"I guess it couldn't be prevented, I mean, who could guess Guzman would break the pattern and do this?" McGlick did not sound convinced by his own logic, and Tony added nothing to what had been said.

"Some things happen that way," McGlick continued, and then let his voice die away. "You heard about Ryan?" he asked, changing the subject. Tony nodded again.

"Think that'll make him put in his retirement papers?" McGlick asked as he went and sat down behind his desk.

"I don't see that he has much choice now," Tony said wearily.

"It'll be better if he just quits," said McGlick. "That means no trial, no anything. He just goes."

"That's up to him," Tony replied. He no longer cared. For him, everything was over. This was a chase he no longer cared to be a part of. Ryan might or might not take the easy way out. If he didn't or if complications developed, McGlick would continue his pursuit of the man to his grave. He was that kind of hunter. It was either McGlick or Ryan, and McGlick took care of McGlick. Whatever happened, Tony would still be the visible agent to the Hirschels, the Galluccis, and the Trataglias. Whatever happened, McGlick was screened by Tony's silence. Because of his ego and reputation, Tony wouldn't talk, even if it meant jail. If anything now went sour, Tony would be the scapegoat.

It was time, he knew, to get off the moving train. He had made his decision.

"Inspector," Tony finally said, "I'm going downtown to put in my retirement papers." McGlick's eyes slitted; his nostrils flared. He remained silent a moment, undecided about how to react. Disapproval was etched across his face, his contempt quite evident.

"Running scared, huh," he finally scoffed.

"No, Inspector," said Tony thoughtfully, "I've just realized something. Twenty years ago, the death of some Puerto Rican by a rapist or the death of a Ryan wouldn't affect a cop. But cops have changed. People have changed, Inspector. They won't let you get away with these things anymore. And you know something, Inspector, I'm glad."

McGlick jumped to his feet. "You little guinea bastard—run—run—for your life."

Without replying, Tony walked from McGlick's office, grabbed some forms from the cabinet, and headed downtown.

McGlick slumped onto the couch in his office. He was confused. What the hell's happening to me? he thought. Wait a second. I'm the tough, honest cop. I'm doing the right thing, damn it. Sure, I have to do shitty things. But it's the bottom line that counts. "That's what counts," he mumbled, over and over. McGlick didn't notice his incredulous clerical lieutenant appear then disappear at the office door.

Tony handed the papers to the clerk at the pension section. He waived his vacation and terminal leave. He wanted out—tonight at midnight. Once out, his pension was secure. If they grabbed him after that, at least he had his pension. As he waited, Tony nervously checked the door behind him. At any moment, he expected McGlick to charge in with two men and arrest him. For what? He didn't know. But he was sure that McGlick would come up with something. Maybe he'd send IAD or maybe Yates would send his men. He desperately wanted to get out of the building. What's taking the clerk so long? he wondered. The clerk was on the phone. Shit, maybe something is wrong, he thought.

It seemed an eternity, but finally, the clerk walked over and said, "Okay, you're cleared—you're out at midnight." Tony sighed and flew out the door. Upon reaching Baxter Street, he felt a ton lighter, free from all the dirty work he had so willingly performed. His pension could no longer be used as a weapon against him, not by McGlick, not by IAD, not by the DA. It was an exhilarating feeling.

✻   ✻   ✻

Joey walked quietly into the office where his father was sprinkling the house plants.

"Did you hear about Ryan's son?" Joey softly asked.

"I heard."

"Well, aren't we going to do something?" Joey asked, somewhat confused.

The don waved his son to a tan leather sofa and sat down beside him. "Joey, Joey," he said in a weary voice, "I've told you before, Patrolman Ryan and his son no longer exist for us. We gave our word to the council and the Triumvirate. We can no longer interfere." The don sighed deeply and continued, "Patrolman Ryan understands this. He knows it is now in his own hands. Believe me, he doesn't think badly of us."

Joey had some difficulty accepting this. Trataglia understood. Most of the younger Mafioso had trouble comprehending the sudden finality and cold logic of the business.

Trataglia decided to blunt the sharp edge for his son. "It took Patrolman Ryan fifty years before he needed a favor returned. Maybe in another fifty years, someone from his family will come to see you for a favor. I expect you to help him." The don smiled. "Good enough?"

"Good enough," Joey answered.

23

THE NEWS WAS not unexpected, but it hurt anyway. Adler had been dumped. Somewhere in the back of his mind, Adler had presupposed that Chief Atmont would prevail over McGlick. This failure, he believed, meant that headquarters wasn't satisfied with his performance either. Adler knew he was competent. The men in the precinct knew it. The borough chief knew it. So what is with those bastards downtown? he wondered. From being the CO of the high-hazard Three-nine Precinct, he was being demoted to a low-prestige administrative job in the property clerk's office. After so many good years in the department, it was time to consider retirement, he decided. For all practical purposes, he had no future in the New York City Police Department. For some men, the captain's salary was enough. They would collect as many checks as they could before being chased out, but Adler was a man of pride and dignity; he wouldn't remain where he felt unwanted. The chief inspector had counted on this side of Adler's personality; shrewd men can use a man's strength against him.

Before leaving the Bronx for the last time, Adler had Detective Davis drive him to Royal Hospital on the Grand Concourse. Ryan had been transferred there from Harlem Hospital that morning. Adler had the strange feeling that their destinies were interwoven, that some higher power had thrown them into the same crucible and their fates were inexorably linked. Whatever happened to Ryan affected him, and whatever happened to him affected Ryan.

Their visit was an unexpectedly emotional one. They hugged each other, two decent men who had shared only professional goals but who each now perceived the finality of this encounter. Davis was moved witnessing the show of affection, although he didn't completely understand it. Davis was still at the hunter level; Ryan and Adler were the hunted. Eventually, the conversation drifted to the rapist.

"The Latent Print Section has linked the homicide with at least one of the rapes already," said Adler. "The big question is, to whom do they belong?"

"How about the guy being a cop?" asked Hugh.

Adler winked. "We have already checked all our cops—and bosses," he said. "It was a tough job, too. They had to be scanned manually."

Davis was smiling. "I'm glad you included the brass this time," he said, looking sideways at Adler.

The captain remembered the case. "Right," said Adler. "The guy turned out to be a lieutenant. It would have saved a lot of grief."

The conversation had triggered Adler's memory. That morning, he told them, a patrolman named Van Buren had reported to him how a "John" had come out of a building on 138th Street shortly before the homicide. Davis nodded, scribbled the name on a pad, and glanced at his watch. The young detective, Adler realized, wanted to get back to the chase. And I have a few good-byes to say, he thought. Oh God, I hope Tucci doesn't ask too many questions. It was time to leave. They wished Ryan well and left. Hugh Ryan smiled. He knew the world would continue to turn, even though for him, it seemed to have stopped.

After dropping Adler at the station house, Davis telephoned Hirschel. Getting no response, he decided to seek out Van Buren.

"Yeah, it was last night around 4:15 AM," said Dutch. "I observed this guy leave 475 East 138th Street and head up Cypress towards Saint Mary's Park. What do you think?"

"The time fits," said Davis with some excitement. "It also fits in with some info I have." He grabbed the telephone and dialed the Latent Print Section while talking.

It only took fifteen minutes, once the sergeant at Latent grasped the significance of the call and located Davis's investigative request. The thumbprint from the knife matched a print found at the scene of one of the rapes. Grabbing Dutch by the arm, Davis led him into the squad commander's office. There was enough glory in this one for all of them.

Anyone entering 475 wouldn't suspect that anything unusual was going on. If they did, there were two detectives in the rear, two on the roof, and two unobtrusively stationed in front of the house to prevent a discerning suspect from fleeing the trap.

When Hirschel had failed to answer his phone, Davis figured he was probably up at McDarby's priming some chick for a midnight date. He was certain, however, that once Hirschel hit the precinct at four o'clock and heard the news, he would fly to the scene, since, as Davis fathomed last night, Hirschel had a special hatred for this guy.

The canvass proceeded slowly upward. An initial check with the super had eliminated some apartments, but it was going to take hours to check each and every room. Some people were at work or out shopping or on vacation.

Raoul hadn't responded to the initial knocking, listening instead at the door as the detective spoke to the lady in the next apartment.

"A young Spanish couple live in that apartment with two children," she said. "His wife and children are on vacation in Puerto Rico."

Raoul began to panic. His police training checked that, but he sensed the net was closing. He decided that his best hope was to flee to Puerto Rico. His family's connections there could effectively protect him from extradition. They had done it for his older brother—wanted in Chicago on the charge of maiming a woman. His first problem, however, was to get out of the building. He checked the street. The casual-looking man near the telephone booth and the guy leaning on the car at the opposite side of the doorway were obviously detectives. The rear yard would be covered, he was sure. That left the roof—his specialty. For the last month, he had walked and run silently in the darkness over most in the area. He hoped that even if it was covered, he might make it. He noticed movement in the street below. More detectives had arrived; his time was short.

The hallway was clear as the lean, muscular man nonchalantly strolled to the staircase and climbed the seventeen steps to the roof door. As usual, it was open. His plan was simple; he would dart out the exit door, veer right, race to the building's edge, and, if sensing any pursuit, leap the twenty-five-foot death chasm. Desperate men did those things; civil servants hesitated to perform such feats.

The two detectives stationed on the roof had surveyed it carefully and were certain that the rapist would run left if flushed upward. Although concealed, they were sitting on a crate on the adjoining roof of 477.

Shocked and immobilized, they watched as a man rushed onto the roof and raced right toward certain death. Then, suddenly, the man stopped and looked to his rear. The detectives hadn't budged from their concealment. Again, watching in amazement, they saw the man turn, pull a switchblade, and run in their direction. The detectives tensed. This was their man. When Raoul jumped the two-foot gap onto 477, they were waiting with drawn revolvers.

"Police, freeze!" the burly detective screamed.

Startled, Raoul flung the knife wildly and turned to flee. The butt of the other detective's gun caught Raoul on the back of the neck, catapulting him over the crevice onto the gravel roof of 475. As Raoul attempted to rise, the hefty detective delivered a kick to his ribs while his partner stomped down hard on Raoul's back. Once incapacitated and prone, he was quickly handcuffed and led downstairs.

It didn't take long for Van Buren and Davis to identify Raoul, locate his apartment, and find all the evidence that would be needed by the district attorney to get an indictment. The partial prints at the scenes of the rapes and homicide would ensure the conviction, even without a positive identification from the victims. With Davis's concurrence, an unusually generous act, Dutch took the arrest and started the prisoner's processing.

Hirschel had not reported for duty. The repeated phone calls went unanswered. Davis decided to first assist Van Buren in processing Raoul then headed for Manhattan.

After McDarby's, Davis hit O'Brien's on Fifty-second and Second, then the Coppers, a British pub named for the tinsmiths, not policemen, where they had shared a few brews with an unknown actor named Robert Shaw, then Connelly's on Twenty-third and Third Avenue. He was working his way south to Hirschel's loft on West Thirteenth Street, pub by pub.

Banging on Hirschel's door and receiving no answer, Davis went to the machine shop below the loft and asked Hans, the old German proprietor, for Hirschel's spare key. The owner gave it to anyone who asked. It was a standing order. Hirschel hated to think of an anxious buddy with a girlfriend paying for lodgings. It took all the romance out of an affair.

The enormous front section of the loft was empty. "Hirschel, are you there?" yelled Davis, as he inched toward the rear partition. Peeking gingerly around the screen, as he had learned not to crash in on friends, Davis smiled. Hirschel was out cold on the circular bed.

As he started to shake his partner, he noticed the blood on the quilt, then the huge .38 Special's hole in Hirschel's temple. Before he reacted professionally (bodies were his business after all), Davis spewed forth his tuna salad onto the disk-like bed. As he continually asked himself why, he noticed the letter on the night table. It read: "The man you want is Raoul Guzman. He lives at 475 East 138th Street, Apt. 52. Forgive me." Two thousand dollars were attached to the note.

Davis patched together his partner's deception. He felt betrayed; his partner had taken the money to sit on the rapist. Apparently, the homicide had created so much remorse, guilt, and shame that Hirschel had killed himself. Davis tottered into the skylighted main studio and fell onto a lambskin-covered couch to analyze the catastrophe.

Only one person, to the best of his knowledge, had benefited from the rapist's tardy demise. He wouldn't allow his mind to even mention the name. It was inconceivable. It was horrendous, and to him, it was dangerous to even contemplate that possibility. He knew what had to be done. He destroyed the note and took the two grand. He would mail it to the widowed Puerto Rican woman, anonymously, of course.

The death would be listed as just another suicide of a distraught cop unable to handle the pressure of the job. Later, when Davis heard of Silent Tony's retirement and waiver of his accrued leave on the same day as the suicide, it confirmed his fears. It was the kind of information that cops were sometimes forced to file in their subconscious for fear of the ramifications. It was a simple matter of survival; partners hang together even if one is completely innocent. And as Davis knew, in the NYC Police Department, blacks were hung upside down by their cojones.

✻ ✻ ✻

On one matter, McGlick was delighted. The rapist's capture had relieved him of a difficult task: how to finger Guzman without bringing suspicion upon himself. That was supposed to be Tony's job. However, the fact that Hirschel's partner, Davis, had solved the case worried McGlick.

Had Hirschel fingered Raoul for Davis before committing suicide? What else might Hirschel have said? McGlick had some questions that needed answers.

The funeral had the traditional police honor guard and had been well attended by both the rank and file and the top brass. Yates and McGlick, in full uniform, seemed to wipe tears from their eyes as the cortege slowly and solemnly left the temple to the sounds of "Taps." It was a magnificent charade, of course.

The Hirschel family was distraught over Al's suicide, unable to fathom the reasons for such a drastic act. Detective Davis couldn't provide any clues when he paid his respects at the shiva immediately following the orthodox funeral in Brooklyn. But Davis knew the truth. Alfred Hirschel had taken his life because he could never face his grandfather again.

Mullarky and O'Rorke's Funeral Home on Castle Hill Avenue in the Bronx had closed for the day. The laughter in the preparation room in the basement was a familiar weekly event; Grandpa was visiting his buddies of over fifty years, Ed Mullarky and Jim O'Rorke. The three men, drinking beer and playing pinochle, were undisturbed by the four bodies, all in different stages of the embalming process, cluttering the small room. The only unusual aspect of tonight's game was the reaction of the undertakers to J.B.'s instruction on how to handle his funeral. It was unique, they agreed, but it was probably the only way to handle an old-salt like him.

Silent Tony was nervous as he and his wife boarded the Silver Streak bound for Miami that night. But as the train pulled out of Grand Central Station and gained speed, he knew he had done the right thing. He sensed that the storm wasn't over yet in the Ryan affair, but regardless of what happened now, he would be safe, rich, and free in Florida. He was only partially right.

24

McGLICK, USING one of his standard ploys, directed Davis to be in his office at 9:00 AM on his day off. A tense Davis sat on the hall bench waiting until 5:00 PM to be interviewed, giving him ample time to appreciate the ruthlessness of the man he was about to see. It also allowed the detective plenty of time to assess his position. His partner was dead. The rapist had been captured. Tony had fled the state. Adler had been transferred and destroyed, and Ryan had been hospitalized. There was no point in challenging this man.

Accordingly, Davis, now sitting nervously on the edge of the chair facing the inspector, made sure McGlick was left with the right impression. His cautious answers to McGlick's probing questions were well received.

"You then consider this a case closed by arrest?" said McGlick several times.

"Positively, Inspector," he would reply. "There's absolutely no loose ends on this one, sir."

Davis walked out of the office knowing he had done, maybe not the right thing, but the smart thing. He also knew that if he ever got the chance to screw McGlick without the remote chance of getting hurt himself, he would do it. Davis would join a multi-racial and rapidly expanding cadre of McGlick haters.

McGlick was still unaware of this group. Most cops, those who hadn't been subjected to his intimidating tactics, saw him as a good boss. He beat on prisoners. He never interfered or stopped a business deal, and he never cut himself in on any of the action. What more could anyone ask? Everyone had certain quirks, and to most cops, the good in McGlick outweighed the bad. Downtown was delighted with his performance. The rapist had been caught, and rumors were circulating that he might be the next chief inspector.

McGlick, however, had a more immediate concern: He needed a replacement for Tony, an agent for the Ryan crusade whose silence could be guaranteed. The division's confidential files uncovered a sergeant whose position was extremely perilous. If McGlick followed through on the information gathered on the man's homosexual affairs, he would be fired. The sergeant wasn't in any position to refuse his services to the inspector. He only had sixteen years on the job and couldn't, like Tony, pull a quick vanishing act. McGlick ordered him assigned to the division office.

Lance Rogers had caused quite a stir at his promotion ceremony to sergeant, kissing the police commissioner on the cheek as his gold shield was handed to him, causing the cherubic commissioner to blush. The audience roared in amusement as the new sergeant wiggled off the stage.

Rogers had been a quiet, efficient cop for the ten years before his promotion, but since that ceremony, he had been closely watched, partly due to that incident and particularly due to his growing penchant for visibility. Even the mayor had spotted him in the St. Patrick's Day Parade doing his thing to the whistles of the crowd. The mayor chided the police commissioner, standing next to him on the reviewing stand, for allowing such shenanigans. He was shocked when the PC told him the guy wasn't acting. Rogers was subsequently banned from marching in all parades, transferred to the Bronx, and purposely put under the watchful eye of McGlick in the Seventh Division.

McGlick, being single himself and living in a YMCA since his mother died, had a thing about homosexuals. It was as if he had to prove he wasn't one of them. On one occasion, McGlick threw two white homosexuals out of a second-floor window of a Bronx station house and then charged them with attempted escape. When the story hit the papers, the official version of course, an inordinate number of guests staying at the same YMCA as McGlick quickly checked out.

Rogers feared McGlick both physically and administratively. With only four years to go, he didn't want to jeopardize his pension rights, which would guarantee him enough money to be himself, to act as he wished to act, to be outrageous and unaffected by the whims of some biased employer—in other words, to be free. In that respect, Rogers was but one of thousands of cops who felt the same way; their pension symbolized freedom. You had to be a cop to completely understand the rationale for that kind of thinking. The pension meant more than just economic freedom. Most cops ended up getting another job anyway. It meant that after years of being ordered around, cursed at by your bosses, treated with contempt and disrespect by your own leaders, subjected to political constraints, and restricted in personal dealings with neighbors and others who had offended you, you could finally stand up and tell someone to go to hell without it resulting in a departmental investigation, complaint, or trial. That was the pressure that men nearing retirement felt. They had endured a coercive system for so many years that the fear of pension loss became abnormally symbolic of the possible loss of their pending freedom. Only another cop could fully understand when a cop uttered, "I've put up with this shit for so long that I'd hate to blow it now."

McGlick had found the right man for his next move against the Ryans.

✳ ✳ ✳

Margaret was still there when Dr. Cahill arrived. She had been spending sixteen hours a day at Hugh's side since the attack. Dr. Cahill, a disheveled, bony man, who was somewhat harried because of his dedication and refusal to turn away patients, was noted for his blunt diagnoses and prognostications, which had won him an ever-growing and appreciative practice. The Irish seemed to love bad news delivered directly and honestly.

"He'll live," said Cahill perfunctorily. "Go home and take care of the little ones."

Margaret knew the doctor's ways. "How long?" she asked.

"Well," he said, "that's up to him. He has to lose some weight, cut down on his cigarettes, and most importantly, reduce stress. Bill has told me," said the doctor, "the whole story." He emphasized the latter part of the statement.

They were in the hallway now. "I'd suggest that he request a medical discharge immediately. Unless the stress is reduced quickly, he won't last. He can live for years if he can get out of the police department alive."

The small, thin man then hurried off without waiting for Margaret's reply; another Irishman's wife waited down the hall for his abrupt appraisal. Margaret smiled for the first time in days, such was her confidence in the beloved family doctor. She went back into the room and kissed her sleeping husband then headed for the Number Twenty-seven bus.

THE NEWS OF Ryan's rapid recovery had been well received in most quarters, but not in the Seventh Division office. McGlick decided to have Sergeant Rogers deliver a message. Ryan, he reasoned, had too much going for him: his past record of honesty and excellent performance, his family history, the lack of solid evidence against him, thanks to the Trataglias, and now, his medical condition. It was a tough combination to beat. The only solution was increased psychological pressure, even if it meant disregarding Yates's most recent warnings. Adler had been handled. Hirschel was dead. Tony was heading for Florida and wouldn't honor a subpoena unless extradited, which was, for all practical considerations, impossible in this case. So who could Ryan subpoena? Stevens and Yates were solid, and nobody knew of their involvement anyway.

McGlick was well aware that Rogers was no Tony. The jobs he had lined up for Rogers wouldn't incriminate himself. The worst they could do was show that he was a cruel and callous person. His friends in the DA's office could easily excuse these to a grand jury as part of his tough, honest, and direct approach to police leadership. Certainly, there would be nothing that could lead to an indictment.

Rogers, a thin, nervous man, chain-smoked his way to Royal Hospital. Rogers was the perennial victim. It had been that way throughout his life. He was being used again, this time by McGlick. As a youth, it had been his stepfather, then in his early twenties, his wife, and after the divorce, a succession of male lovers. One sergeant who had worked with him for three years described him as a man he had at first pitied. The guy vacillated on everything. But in time, he came to detest Rogers.

The man seemed to thrive on being degraded, whether it be by superiors, peers, subordinates, or citizens. The investigators found that his respect quotient was zero.

Not knowing Ryan made his task bearable. Following instructions, Rogers waited for Hugh's visitors to leave the room before entering. Obviously nervous, he timidly told Hugh that he had a message to deliver. When Rogers paused inordinately long, a recovering Hugh said with some annoyance, "Well, what the hell is the message?"

Rogers cleared his throat. "I've been told to tell you that the only way you won't go to trial is if you die." He said it in one fast burst.

Hugh could feel his anger rising. Reaching out to grab Rogers, Hugh lost his balance and fell to the floor with a loud thud, ripping out the intravenous connections.

The noise alerted the nurse. As she ran toward the private room, Rogers pushed past her in flight. No immediate damage had been done. Hugh was helped back to bed, and the summoned house surgeon replaced the IV, conducted several tests, and then called Dr. Cahill.

Upon arrival, Dr. Cahill couldn't believe the story recounted to him by Hugh. Although the courier was unknown to Hugh, he had no doubt as to the origin of the message. Hugh insisted that he would forget the incident, but McGlick had scored heavily. If Hugh didn't know it, Dr. Cahill did.

Grandpa answered the phone. He was visibly shaken by the news, grabbing the banister as he slumped to the stairs. Bill noticed the weakness but stayed on the sofa, not wanting to alarm Margaret, who sat in her sewing chair, her back to Grandpa, smoothing her face with Pond's Cold Cream.

Grandpa didn't want to distress Margaret either; it was the first night in weeks that she seemed self-contained and at peace.

"I'm glad to hear that, Doctor," Grandpa said. "You're right, I think it's best if he's moved into a ward."

Dr. Cahill, taken aback for a moment, realized the game the old man was playing and the logic of the move. It would be done, the nurses briefed, and security alerted, he assured him.

McGlick's actions had reached a new low in the annals of police revenge. A contract had never been put out by a cop on another cop to Grandpa's knowledge. The Harlem incident had been a frame, not a contract to kill a cop, although it could have easily resulted in a cop's death. But this action was a deviously devised, premeditated attempt to cause his son to have another heart attack—to kill him.

Grandpa met Bill's later queries with vague answers. He wanted to sleep on the matter. Bill was now used to Grandpa's methods, so it didn't worry him; he would eventually be told what was necessary, but Margaret would never be told of the incident.

IT WAS A BEAUTIFUL morning. There were enough cumulus clouds to break the sun's continuous vigil of the rear yard. The humidity was low, and the garden chairs remained cool. Grandpa had left the house and passed through the ivy-covered trellis into the secluded sitting area protected on both sides by garage walls and in the rear by a fieldstone wall which Hugh had constructed in the forties to protect their victory garden from the indigenous raccoons and rabbits. Flopping down into his favorite lawn chair, he filled his corncob with tobacco, lit it, and slowly drew on the pipe. He was contemplating the unthinkable: the murder of Inspector McGlick. He knew he could easily get to the man to accomplish the deed. He had the guts to do it. So the only item left to be resolved was the moral aspect of the act. Tears came to his eyes remembering his crippled father, shot down by another Irishman in 1863 and then cast aside by the department he had loved as unfit for duty. His father, Matthew Ryan, was the finest man he had known. Unable to perform police duty, he formed a roofing company and was moderately successful, but it was the forgiving, gentle, loving side of the man that brought tears to Grandpa's eyes now. Matthew had testified at Patty O'Rourke's trial that Patty, well known on his beat as a respectable but hot-tempered man, had probably fired the weapon by mistake as the gun had been held toward the ground and had not been pointed at him directly. The judge and prosecutor were shocked by his testimony, but Matthew felt that the truth was the truth; he had no personal malice toward O'Rourke. Matthew's testimony resulted in O'Rourke receiving a lighter sentence. He had treated his children in the same manner: firmly, but with gentleness and love.

Grandpa felt his father's presence today, more than he had in many years. He realized that it was the crisis situation threatening the family; it demanded all possible inputs before any drastic action was undertaken.

Grandpa had been a good man, led a decent Christian life, but he knew he was no equal to his father. The drinking had started after he had been run down by a beer wagon in 1909. With his left shoulder shattered and the arm broken in several places, he nearly died of shock. There were no miracle drugs in 1909 except beer and whiskey; he preferred beer. Fortunately, he often thought, he was a sleeping drunk, not a fighting or nasty one. The stupors hadn't led to any real family problems, though he often regretted the time lost with his lovely wife, Kathleen, the time lost with his children, and the lost chances to love and live life to the fullest. Kathleen had provided the family leadership, handled the burdens, and raised the kids. When she died in 1926, the shock of her death and the children's needs restored him to being a full-time father. Dr. Cahill's father, a caring doctor himself, prescribed a new drug which reduced the pain in his shoulder, though he still enjoyed an occasional quart or two.

Of all his children, and he and Kathleen had six, the dearest and most beautiful, Bernadette, had died shortly after her marriage in 1933. Sara and Eileen had always accepted that special look their father had for Bernadette, as she was a carbon copy of their beloved, departed mother. Hugh had followed in his father's early footsteps and became a cop. Robert had gone to work for Consolidated Edison, and Jack had taken over the family roofing business, moving it, despite Grandpa's ire, to New Jersey of all places. Everyone usually attended all the family reunions, except Jack, who did, however, make the weddings and wakes.

For two hours, Grandpa had pondered the past, present, and future. As if talking to someone, he gently gestured with his pipe and looked upward. The family history, he concluded, had been an honorable if not always smooth one. To murder McGlick would bring disgrace and dishonor to the entire family, and this he could not do. God had given him a second chance to straighten out his own life, provided him with the opportunity to love and help his children, and had blessed him with fun-loving and obedient grandchildren. He couldn't spit in God's face now that he had been dealt a lousy hand. He would win or lose doing what was acceptable in terms of his family's religious beliefs and commitments to the law.

Before supper, Grandpa told Bill that there were two possible ways to save Hugh. The first was to discover a weak link in McGlick's assault tactics; to get something on him. "It's a remote chance, at best," he said. "But let's not rule it out yet," he quickly added. "Your father gave me a list of his friends in the Three-nine. I want you to talk to them. Find out what you can."

The second avenue of escape was for Hugh to request a medical retirement. This seemed a more promising approach since they had the support of Dr. Samuels, the police surgeon, and Dr. Cahill, the family physician. "I'll look into this one myself tomorrow," said Grandpa.

"You know, there's another way," said Bill, looking intently into Grandpa's sad eyes.

"No, Bill, there isn't," said Grandpa abruptly. "God and the law, remember that." Bill was hurt by the brusqueness of the remark but smiled when Grandpa put his arm around his shoulders and bent his head to seek out the young man's eyes.

"I spent two days ruling that out," said Grandpa.

Both men were now grinning.

27

THE SUBWAY TRIP to the medical unit at 246 Broadway had been unusual in only one respect; Grandpa spotted a trail. It didn't upset him. What he intended to do would be a public record within the hour. It was routine. When an officer applied for retirement, all offices in the department were immediately notified. The purpose was to determine if the officer was the subject of a current investigation; if he was, appropriate action would be taken.

The patrolman handling the filing process allowed Grandpa to fill out the required forms after the situation was explained and a notarized statement from his son produced. The application was for a line-of-duty medical retirement. The rationale, which Grandpa outlined in the request, was that Hugh's heart attack had been caused by the Harlem debacle and the machete incident. He also noted that the actual collapse occurred while on duty. Line-of-duty medical retirement meant a tax-free, three-quarter-pay pension, while ordinary medical retirement would mean about half-pay for Hugh. If Hugh was turned down on both of the two possible medical retirements, he would have no alternative, if he wanted a pension, but to serve his final year.

Leaving the building, Grandpa noticed the same man in a phone booth engaged in animated conversation. Grandpa waved to him. Rogers hung up and followed. For the fun of it, Grandpa gave Rogers the slip on the subway platform applying the in-out-in routine, leaving Rogers standing flatfooted at the station as the train pulled away.

Hugh had come home. The crepe streamers and "Welcome Home" signs cheered him, but he didn't feel like celebrating. He was anxious to get on with the battle. He waited impatiently for Grandpa's return from headquarters.

28

HEADQUARTERS CHIEFS, borough commanders, and division inspectors all had informers within the units under their command. Most police officers were extremely circumspect in verbalizing their complaints or personal opinions. When they did, it was in low tones and tight circles and for good reason. Open and emotionally honest cops were usually subjected to reconditioning by "the system" and then sent to hellish precincts designated for misfits. Before his career ended, Bill Ryan would pay dearly for his refusal to hide his true feelings and opinions. Although he reluctantly acknowledged the curse publicly, inwardly, he saw it as a virtue; he simply enjoyed mocking the hypocrisy and egomania that surrounded him.

McGlick had received the informant's call himself. Bill Ryan had visited the Three-nine Precinct looking for help. The news only increased McGlick's annoyance with the Ryans. He was growing impatient. He wanted the damn thing resolved and ended. He dialed headquarters. Yates, interrupted while making his own retirement plans by McGlick's call, also wanted it settled prior to his retirement for two reasons: He had a bargain to uphold, and he was afraid of what McGlick might do if he didn't honor the commitment. Yates sensed that his power to control McGlick was waning, and he was the only man in the department who could.

✳ ✳ ✳

One officer who heard of Bill's visit was Dutch Van Buren, not a friend of Sergeant Ryan's, but a subordinate who shared a common distaste for the division inspector's methods. After talking it over with his fellow dissidents, it was agreed that their complaints and testimony might be of value to Ryan. It was decided, however, that prior to irrevocably committing themselves to Ryan's cause, they would wait to see which direction the case took. They could not afford to back a loser. It was suicidal.

✳   ✳   ✳

Grandpa was surprised. Hugh was ordered to appear before the medical board tomorrow—the board's first meeting in September. Cops usually had to wait weeks after filing their application before getting an appointment to appear for a physical evaluation. Such preferential treatment was ordinarily reserved for police commissioners and chiefs. Hugh's attendance had been cleared by both Dr. Samuels and Dr. Cahill, the notification indicated.

An atmosphere of cautious optimism prevailed that night in the big house. Everyone was holding their collective breath, for if they got lucky, Hugh could be a free man by twelve noon tomorrow. Margaret took a walk after supper with Grandpa. Without discussing their route, they arrived at the altar of the Nativity Church; each deposited a quarter into the slot of the offering box, lit a candle, and prayed a common prayer.

Raoul Guzman, incarcerated at the Bronx House of Detention awaiting his murder trial, was also engaged in prayer. The ones he offered, however, were for himself. Raoul had been threatened with the electric chair by the Bronx district attorney. In an unusual move, the local Spanish daily newspapers had likewise supported the death penalty for Raoul. Only time would tell whose prayers, if any, would be answered.

HUGH ATE THE small bowl of oatmeal with skim milk in silence. There was no need for conversation; all present felt the tension building, the anticipation growing, the hope incubating. "My God," said Margaret to Bill, after having kissed Hugh and Grandpa good-bye with false courage and watching the old car back down the driveway, "what will happen if they turn him down?"

"No way they can," said Bill supportively, realizing, however, that it was a distinct possibility.

Uniquely, Grandpa had no advice for Hugh during the trip. Today's decision had already been made, nothing could alter it now. He only hoped that someone of decency had intervened, sick of watching the deadly leeching of his son.

There were several men, obviously cops, sitting on benches outside the room where the medical board met. Their faces were expressionless. Another officer, in a wheelchair, his right leg noticeably atrophied, sat off to the side with his wife standing motionless and erect behind him. Hugh took a spot on one of the benches. He looked at those around him. They were all either staring straight ahead blankly or scanning the floor as if able to read shoes. All heads turned, however, when the sound of rolling casters was heard down the hall. A man, lying on his back on a mechanic's sled, was propelling himself toward them, a uniformed cop following closely behind. The man, a cop who had been shot in the back several years earlier, stopped the sled beyond the staging area and just parked there, waiting like all the rest to be examined by the board of doctors.

A short police officer with a stub of a DiNapoli cigar stuffed in the corner of his mouth opened the door immediately in front of the group and yelled, "Patrolman Donovan." The wheelchair started to move. The shaking woman rolled her husband into the examination room.

About this time, a distinguished-looking gentleman in a tailored suit came down the hall. Most present recognized him as Chief O'Brien from Manhattan North. O'Brien, oblivious to the gazes, opened the door forcibly and marched inside. After a few minutes, a second door opened down the hall and O'Brien emerged with a short, thin man with thick glasses close on his heels. Hugh had taken a half-smoked Pall Mall from his shirt pocket and lit it. His curiosity piqued, he got up and simulated an aimless amble to arrive within strained hearing distance of the two men now engaged in whispered conversation. He caught the important part. "You got it, Chief, three-quarters," said the small man with glasses. O'Brien patted the man on the back.

"Thanks, Dr. Rich, I appreciate the help," said O'Brien with a broad grin. He then rushed off to catch the opened elevator.

Going back to the bench, Hugh had hope. Maybe this was the good board, the all-approving board, which rumor had sitting only once each month. That dream was punctured quickly when a screaming woman pushed the wheelchair with a crying officer out the second door down the hall. Several officers, including Hugh, went to the aid of the hysterical woman. "They said he refused treatment," she screamed, as if pleading for justice from those assembled. "Our doctor said the operation might do more harm than good!" she cried. "How could we take that chance?"

Hugh left and let the other officers comfort the distraught woman when he heard someone calling, "Sergeant Ryan, Sergeant Ryan."

Hugh entered the examination room and was waved to a chair in front of a long table. He could still hear the commotion in the hall, the woman crying, "How can they do this to us?" The three doctors hadn't lifted their heads. They were looking at the folders in front of them. Dr. Rich introduced himself. "I'm Dr. Rich," he said, intently studying Hugh. "This is Dr. Ranji, and this is Dr. Bush." The other doctors, each apparently in their seventies, didn't bother to look up. Dr. Rich, who was in his early fifties, rose from his chair and walked from behind the table as might a prosecuting attorney about to interrogate a hostile witness. "Now, Sergeant Ryan, you claim you've had a heart attack?" said Rich. "Is that correct?"

"Yes, sir, that's correct," said Hugh. "I think that the hospital records and Dr. Cahill's letter substantiate the fact."

"Well, let's assume you did have a heart attack," said Rich, "although at the present time, the board is not as certain about that as you seem to be."

"I think the record—" said Hugh, before being interrupted by Rich.

"I said, 'let's assume you did,'" said Rich. "To what do you attribute it?"

"I had the attack on the job, so I attribute it to the job," said Hugh, looking at the other doctors for support, but they still had their eyes on the folders.

"Are you suggesting to this board," said Rich, "that the pressure of patrol caused you to have a heart attack?"

"Yes, I am," said Hugh firmly.

"Since July, how many days have you been the sergeant on patrol?" asked Rich with contempt. He didn't wait for an answer. "Isn't it true that you've only been on such patrol several times in the last two months?"

"That's true, but for five years—" said Hugh. Once again, he was stopped.

"You're only fifty years old," said Rich.

"That's right," said Hugh angrily. The attitude of Dr. Rich was irritating him.

"Well, the board feels that even if you have what you claim you have," said Rich, "it's not due to your job. And to be candid, the board doesn't feel that you have had a heart attack."

Hugh had had enough. "Is that what you really believe?" he said. "What about you, Dr. Ranji? What about you, Dr. Bush?" Neither doctor bothered to respond, continuing to ignore the applicant.

"You guys are really something," said Hugh. "Why don't you examine me?"

"I think that we have stated our professional view, Sergeant," said Rich. "You can leave now."

"You've really been well instructed," said Hugh with sarcasm.

"Sergeant, the board feels that you are fit for full duty," said Rich. "You can stand trial."

Hugh, though stunned by the cruelty of the statement, struck back. "So that's what this rush treatment is all about, you stinkin' hypocrites!" he yelled.

"I see why you have enemies in high places," said Rich.

"You're a bunch of hit men, not doctors!" yelled Hugh.

"Sergeant," yelled Rich, "if you don't leave immediately, we will make an official complaint on you."

Hugh, the pain rising in his chest, was determined not to let the police department kill him. Taking one of Dr. Cahill's pills, he staggered out of the room to seek a glass of water.

The sight of Hugh's bloodless face was enough to alert Grandpa to what had transpired upstairs. A tear came to his eyes as he threw his arms around his son. "They've beat us, son," he said. "You can't beat the organization. I think the only sensible thing left to do is to quit. You can't take another year of this. I can't. Margaret can't. The family can't. I've never been so sorry that I persuaded you to take this job as I am right now."

Dr. Samuels had had a busy morning between catering to an unusual swarm of sick officers and the phone calls. The extra medical duties had been handled with calmness and concern, but two of the calls had caused irritation. The first distressing conversation had been with the chief surgeon, who suggested that Ryan be returned to duty forthwith. The doctor refused outright to acquiesce to the request and hung up on the chief surgeon. A few minutes later, he slammed down the phone on an irate Chief Inspector Yates, after informing Yates that police politics did not mix well with medical care. Dr. Cahill's call had been treated respectfully. The family doctor had been upset at the lack of good faith shown by the medical section. He had been assured that Ryan would be treated in such a manner as not to aggravate his condition.

"The big guns are out to get him," said Samuels, being quite candid with his professional colleague. "There's no way that I can see to protect him indefinitely. I'm not sure that he can survive a trial, and I'll tell you this, they will never let him out without that trial."

After hanging up, Dr. Cahill sat, absorbing what he had been told. The advice he had given to the Ryans last night had been reaffirmed. If Ryan went to trial, he would probably be convicted and dismissed from the department. Even if he beat the charges in the trial room, the ordeal presented, in his professional opinion, a 90 percent chance of another attack and certain death. It was an absolute no-win situation for Ryan. He had to quit, pension or no pension.

McGlick was angered by the news from Yates that Surgeon Samuels was unwilling to cooperate on this routine disciplinary case. But McGlick had a counter-strategy for most situations, which was one reason for Yates's deep-seated fear of the man. Yates, assured a largesse on the Adler matter and certain of a tax-free, three-quarter pension due to his leg, desperately wanted to leave a contented McGlick behind him. Yates had been ruthless at times during his career—all top brass possessed that capability—but for McGlick, it was a relentless, uncontrollable instinct in which he took great personal pride. Lately, McGlick enjoyed saying, "Thank God I have the killer instinct. When justice demands it, I always go for the jugular." This was the overriding reason why Yates didn't want to cross McGlick. The man had become a vindictive psycho.

So when McGlick offered an alternative strategy, one so simple that Yates was annoyed that he hadn't concocted it himself, Yates readily accepted it. Under McGlick's plan, the chief surgeon would assign Samuels to the medical section for weekend duty and have another, properly selected surgeon cover Samuels' district temporarily.

Yates, his uneasiness rising, made the call to the chief surgeon immediately. Yates was now as vulnerable as a rookie walking his first beat in the Seventh Division, and both men knew it.

Rogers had reported in by phone that there had been no movement in or out of the Ryan house, with the exception of Dr. Cahill. Grandpa was still the threat, so Rogers' orders remained unchanged: If the old man left, follow him. McGlick realized that the shadowing ploy hadn't been effective. Rogers had been sighted on the first day, and it didn't appear to have unnerved the old man. The inspector toyed with a variation on the theme; maybe an indirect attack, such as shadowing his grandson, would have greater impact on his seasoned opponent. McGlick smiled. "This will do it," he snickered. He picked up the phone and dialed Yates's number. Yates wasn't expecting another assignment. He reluctantly accepted his subordinate's latest request, which, although asked in a friendly and almost fawning manner, really constituted an order. This most recent demand unnerved Yates, but he had no recourse other than to comply.

That afternoon, Hugh was ordered to appear at his district surgeon's office the next morning. Margaret told Hugh to advise the doctor of his decision to quit the department. Grandpa planned to drive Hugh to the surgeon and then, barring any unforeseen circumstances, drive Hugh to the Forty-seventh Precinct, where he would turn in his gun and shield and fill out the required forms. A pension is no good to a dead man.

Yates, constantly decrying McGlick's growing ruthlessness to himself, hadn't been much kinder to Adler, transferring him three times already. Adler had been to the Ninth in Manhattan and the 103rd in Queens. He was now going to the 122nd on Staten Island. Next week, Yates hoped to send him to the Seventy-third in Brooklyn. The transfers, justified to the police commissioner as attempts to rid the department of a poor commander by harassing him into retirement, had had the desired effect on Adler and his wife. It was Adler's opinion that after the first transfer, he would be forgotten. But Yates's deal with the Galluccis, unknown to Adler, required Adler's retirement before any payment was made. He would not be forgotten.

30

ON NIGHTS HE couldn't sleep, since he didn't drink or have a weeknight female friend, McGlick had only one option—gyms not being open—and that was to ride. It was 3:00 AM, and he was hawking the Forty-second Precinct. Someone has to break balls, he assured himself. What else will keep these bums awake and sober?

Everyone was on his toes. If McGlick was seen on the west side of the precinct, the sergeants headed for the east side; if he went north, they went south. McGlick was aware of this avoidance pattern whenever he rode, but tonight, he found it particularly irksome. There was one place where they couldn't elude him. He headed for the station house.

Directly across the street from the Four-two Precinct was Muldoon's Saloon, a haven for off-duty cops and, not infrequently, on-duty station house personnel. Tonight's prey, if McGlick got his wish, would be the desk officer, a new sergeant named Quinn, who had transferred in from Queens with the reputation of a guy who enjoyed a highball.

McGlick parked his car on Westchester Avenue, a block from the station house. After creeping around the corner and up the front stairs of the Four-two, he charged into the muster room shouting, "Where's Quinn? Where's Quinn?"

The only person in the room at the time, the half-sober telephone operator, shakily told McGlick, "Sergeant Quinn is out inspecting the perimeter of the station house for bombs." McGlick turned without debating the point and raced toward Muldoon's.

151

An off-duty officer looking out of Muldoon's front window spotted the stalking inspector. "The Brim!" he yelled, which was sufficient threat and warning to send Quinn and several other off-post cops wobbling to the rear alley. From there, they could reach the back door of the precinct within a minute.

The telephone switchboard operator, unaware that the alarm had already been sounded, dialed Muldoon's. The phone booth line was still ringing when the wild-eyed inspector aggressively entered the pub. The unperturbed atmosphere convinced him that he had been outmaneuvered, but his uncanny instincts made him rush to the phone booth, outdistancing the ambling bartender. Quickly picking up the receiver, he said, "Yeah?"

"Tell Quinn to get the hell out of there. That crazy bastard McGlick is heading that way," said the voice.

"Okay," said McGlick, "hold on for a second." He waved to the bartender. "It's for me," said McGlick. "Hold it, but don't hang up." Sprinting back across the street, McGlick silently entered the house. The telephone operator, phone to ear, was too engaged to notice him. Ripping the phone from the officer's hand, McGlick spoke into it. "This is the precinct. Is this Muldoon's?"

"Yeah," said the bartender. Then he added, grasping the situation, "Oh shit, The Brim is coming at you fast."

"Well, hang up Muldoon, this is The Brim!" screamed McGlick into the speaker. He slammed the phone down. Quinn was behind the desk now, writing in the blotter that his perimeter bomb inspection had been negative. McGlick scowled, threatened, intimidated, ranted, and raved for twenty minutes before ordering both men to be in his office at nine o'clock that morning following their tour of duty.

McGlick had worked off his excessive energy; he could sleep now, so he headed back toward the YMCA on 161st Street, but before he reached his lodgings, a report from the Seventh Division radio alerted him that a child molester had been apprehended and was being brought into the Three-nine Precinct. Although weary, McGlick couldn't pass up the thought of getting a piece of a pervert.

When he arrived at the Three-nine, McGlick observed a small Puerto Rican standing next to a patrolman in front of the desk talking to the lieutenant. He didn't waste a second; he pounced on the man, threw him to the floor, and stomped him repeatedly with his steel-toed shoes until the officer, realizing that the small man was already unconscious, pleaded with and begged the inspector to stop. After a few more kicks, the persuasion worked.

"The dirty bastard child molester," said McGlick. "He deserved it."

The lieutenant, visibly shaken by the attack, said nervously, "Sir, the man was just asking for directions—the degenerate hasn't arrived yet."

McGlick was taken aback only for a moment. He looked at the inert officer. "Well, just don't stand there!" he shouted. "Lock him up for assaulting a police officer." McGlick turned and left.

The arrest was made.

✳ ✳ ✳

The note on Dr. Samuels' door read: "All officers report to Surgeon Frost at 2487 Grand Concourse." It was 8:30 AM when Grandpa and Hugh, rerouted by the note, arrived at the fill-in surgeon's office. When Hugh's turn came, Grandpa went into the examination room with him. He wasn't taking any chances today. Dr. Frost ordered Grandpa to wait outside. Grandpa refused. The doctor relented.

"I see here," said Frost, "that you were examined by the medical board yesterday and found fit for duty. Dr. Rich reports that your pressure was normal, 130 over 90, that after a minute of exercise, your heart sounded fine, and that your pressure rose substantially but within normal limits. It's his opinion that you might only have a hiatus hernia."

Grandpa grabbed Hugh by the arm. "Would you believe that my son was never even examined by Dr. Rich?" said Grandpa with disdain. Hugh was incredulous.

"Let's not get ridiculous," said Frost. "Your son is fit for duty. Sergeant Ryan, you are returned to duty effective midnight on the fifth."

Once again, Grandpa grasped his son's arm. "Let's go, Hugh," he said. "We know what we have to do."

The phone call to the Ryan home had come shortly after 8:00 AM. Bill, preparing to attend a three-day vehicular training course, spoke to the caller, Dutch Van Buren. Dutch told Bill about the merciless beating administered by McGlick earlier to the innocent bystander. Bill wasn't sure how this affected his father's predicament. McGlick has been able to stifle the family's investigation at every turn so far, he thought. Why should this be any different? Bill decided, however, to leave the analysis and decision-making to his father and grandfather. Receiving no answer at Dr. Samuels' number, Bill, aware of their itinerary, called the Forty-seventh Precinct and left a message for his father. Sensing he might be needed, Bill then called the police academy to request an emergency day off. The sergeant on duty granted it. He would later be transferred to Brooklyn as a result of that kindness. Sitting in the kitchen studying his notebook, Bill waited.

Hugh, given the message and the required forms at the Four-seven desk, asked Grandpa to check with Bill while he went into the sitting room to start filling out the resignation papers.

Grandpa sensed a new life-death choice emerging when Bill told him of McGlick's most recent misadventure. It presented a great opportunity, if exploited immediately and with finesse. But every minute, every hour, and every day that Hugh remained under the gun, his life was in jeopardy. Grandpa acknowledged that the intense fight had weakened him, too.

The two men sat in the sitting room, two weary warriors conversing in whispered tones on their best course of action. They eventually rejected the course which each man now knew was best, resignation, deciding instead to blitz McGlick on his latest error, hoping that downtown would shy away from the organizational kill and permit Hugh to retire without a trial. If within forty-eight hours, they agreed, no substantial progress had been made to achieve that goal, Hugh would resign.

The desk lieutenant, surprised to see them walking out, yelled, "Change of heart?"

"We decided to wait awhile," said Hugh, the strain evident in his cracking voice.

Upon returning home, Grandpa carefully instructed Bill as to what had to be done. It was up to the young man now. Both Grandpa and Hugh had used up, at least for the day, their reserve supply of fortitude. Weeks earlier, Hugh would have vetoed Bill's mission, but after being subjected to such harsh treatment by his beloved department, he readily agreed with Grandpa's tactics.

Margaret, upon learning of the change in plans, and still wanting Hugh's immediate resignation, uncharacteristically and vehemently challenged their logic. She also chided Bill for not telling her about the earlier call. It was an emotional response, her intuition telling her that nothing positive would be gained by another assault on the establishment. She was frightened. She, more than the men, realized what was involved here; it was their male egos. That was what frightened her. She knew that as long as a chance of victory, however slim, remained, her competitive husband and father-in-law would continue to fight even if it meant death. She cursed to herself, wishing her men could accept inevitable defeat with grace and peace. Didn't their religion teach them that? But Margaret was also wise. She knew that their actions weren't a repudiation of her, the children, or their religion, but a reaffirmation of their real view on life. To Grandpa and Hugh, life emulated sport; they firmly believed that no fight, baseball game, or race was over until the final bell, out, or line had been rung, made, or crossed respectively. She had admired that trait for years. Now she dreaded it.

31

THE BRONX CRIMINAL COURT, located at 161st Street and Third Avenue, was a clean-lined and impressive building; what made it dirty were the deals, frauds, and evils perpetrated in its halls, bathrooms, cubicles, cells, and sometimes even its courtrooms. Most of the lawyers operating in and around this citadel of justice would never become Supreme Court justices, which augured well for the country. But many would, unfortunately, become city leaders. The lesson learned here—that anything can be purchased for a price—would eventually lead to the ruin of the Bronx. But in the meantime, business was business.

Bill had checked the calendar posted in the second-floor hallway; Hector Rodriguez, McGlick's assault victim, would be arraigned in part 1A charged with assault-two on a police officer. Bill sat near the front of the courtroom close to the bench to make sure he spotted his man; the constant buzz in the courtroom made audibility beyond the third row impossible. Right behind Bill, a lawyer was talking to his client's wife. "The price is fifty dollars," said the lawyer coldly.

"I'll give you twenty dollars now, thirty next week," said the Puerto Rican woman. "That's all I have."

"Yeah, all right," the lawyer said. The woman got up and went back to her family. Out of the corner of his eye, Bill saw the lawyer wave to another client's wife. The conversation was similar to the first. The procedure continued again and again as the bailiff called the cases. A second man stopped briefly and asked, "How are you doing today?"

"Pretty good so far," he responded, "but I have to have these three cases held on no bail until I get paid. You know how these bastards are." He handed the man an envelope. "Give this to the court clerk." The second man smiled and walked past the judge's bench into a rear office.

The bailiff yelled, "Patrolman Jenson, Case of Hector Rodriguez." Rodriguez was led limping and bent into the courtroom by a court officer. Patrolman Jenson approached the bench from the public area pushing open the swinging gate and taking his position to the right of the prisoner in front of the judge. The public defender, assigned by the Legal Aid Society, which provided counsel for indigents, informed the court that he represented the prisoner.

"You're charged with assaulting an officer of the law," said the judge. "How do you plead?"

"He pleads not guilty, Your Honor," said the defense attorney.

"Trial date?" asked the judge. The officer conferred with Rodriguez's lawyer.

After several moments, the public defender spoke, "We have agreed on the seventh, fourteenth, or seventeenth of September, Your Honor."

"Make it the seventh," said the judge. "No bail." He nodded to the prisoner's attorney. The lawyer got the message and now conferred with his client. He told Rodriguez that if, after his trial on the seventh, he was found guilty, that the time spent in jail up to that date would constitute his complete sentence. It was emphasized to Rodriguez that he would go free on that date whether he was found innocent or guilty. The defendant was confused by the logic involved but accepted at his attorney's urging. In essence, the judge had found him guilty already; it saved time and paperwork to do it this way. The public defender agreed.

Rodriguez was removed to a waiting pen from which he would be taken in several hours by the Department of Corrections and lodged in one of their facilities until his day in court.

It was time for Bill to make his move. He took a deep breath, pinned his shield onto his breast pocket, and strutted authoritatively into the clerk's office. He had never done anything like this before. He hoped he would never have to do it again. Upon entering the room, Bill immediately shook hands with the clerk, who deftly removed the five-dollar bill from Bill's cupped fingers.

"I'm working on a case," said Bill. "I'd like to talk to that Rodriguez guy. Hector is the first name."

"Sure," said the greased clerk pleasantly. "Go right through that door; he's in the pen."

"By the way," said Bill, shaking hands with the clerk again. "If the guy makes a statement, would you notarize it for me?" The clerk's face creased into a broad grin. Bill wondered how many times this guy extended his right paw each day; he must have a golden hand by now.

"Just call me," said the clerk, turning suddenly to greet another visitor.

Hector Rodriguez, a small, light-brown man who spoke understandable but broken English, engulfed in disbelief already, was further confused by Bill's questions. Naturally suspicious after the strange events of the last twelve hours, Rodriguez was hesitant to cooperate with any gringo. This was the first time he had been arrested, the first day of work he had missed since coming to New York five years earlier, the first night he had spent away from his family, and the first time in his life that he felt demeaned and abused. It took some time before Bill finally succeeded, as he couldn't guarantee Rodriguez anything for his statement other than the fact that it would aid Bill's father who had been similarly victimized.

As Bill printed out the man's story verbatim, he cringed in disgust, empathizing with the man's plight. At its best, a terrible mistake had occurred, but rather than correcting the error, McGlick had compounded it, further punishing an innocent man. Bill asked the clerk to step into the cell block to witness the signing of the statement. To discourage any reservations on the clerk's part and to prevent his reading the document, Bill had his strategy prepared which, in truth, had Grandpa's touch to it. After Rodriguez signed the document, Bill held the paper on the waist-level shelf used to hold prisoners' belts, ties, and other possibly self-destructive-type property with his left hand covering most of the statement, while his right hand was busy stuffing another bill into the clerk's left pants pocket. The clerk was smiling once again as he affixed his seal to the document. It was done. The clerk hurried off.

Bill asked Rodriguez if he could do anything for him, get him cigarettes, call his wife, his job, whatever. The man started to weep, weakly at first and then deep, uncontrollable sobs. Bill waited in understanding silence as the man attempted to regain his composure.

"Please, please," he said, wiping his eyes, "tell my wife, tell my children, it's not my fault."

Bill would stop at the man's Kelly Street apartment later on that day, but his immediate task, perhaps more difficult than the one just completed, was to get an audience with the police commissioner.

Using the East River Drive, which was lightly traveled early in the afternoon, enabled Bill to reach his exit at Grand Street in twenty minutes. Five minutes later, he parked the family Packard on Centre Street directly across from the entrance to headquarters.

Entering the police commissioner's rotunda and waiting room had intimidated more prominent men than Bill Ryan. Although awed by the room, in which a picture of Teddy Roosevelt was strategically displayed to be seen immediately upon entry, Bill reminded himself that this was no time for his resolve to weaken.

The detective lieutenant serving as the PC's receptionist used various bureaucratic techniques to sidetrack the young officer. "Did you make a written request to see the PC? Did you go through channels with your complaint? Does your commanding officer know you're here? If you're a recruit, how come you're not in class?"

Bill answered each question honestly, emphasizing that the matter concerned his father, that time was of the utmost importance, and that the seriousness of the situation required a prompt decision from the PC. The lieutenant was annoyed that even after prolonged questioning, Bill still refused to divulge the exact nature of his complaint. Bill waited as the receptionist-bodyguard made numerous trips in and out of the commissioner's office. No doubt, Bill realized, the telephone lines to various commands throughout the department were buzzing, searching for answers as to why this persistent rookie desperately wanted to talk to the commissioner.

It is an unusual bureaucrat who will see a distantly removed subordinate, especially one who has bypassed the insular and protective levels of the hierarchy. It would have to be a well-checked-out and extraordinary set of circumstances to honor such a request. The PC finally decided, after several hours of investigation by his staff and against their advice, to talk briefly to young Ryan. Bill was ushered into the commissioner's office. He walked directly to the PC's desk, stood at attention, and saluted.

"Probationary Patrolman Ryan, reporting as directed, sir," recited Bill. How to enter a superior's office was one of the first things they drilled you on in the academy.

Police Commissioner O'Grady, who was average sized with a receding hair line and pockmarked face, was always uncomfortable in his dealings with the rank and file. He had found it advisable in the recent past to adhere to strict protocol.

"At ease, Officer," he said matter-of-factly. "I've reviewed your father's case, perfunctorily, of course," he said quickly. To always leave yourself an out was a bureaucratic must. "If you have any new evidence or whatever," said the PC, "I've designated the chief inspector to look into it."

"But, sir, you have to hear me out," said Bill urgently. "My grandfather said to only trust the commissioner."

Suddenly, a frightened look crossed the commissioner's face. He remembered—the wiretapping in the Bronx, the old retired cop, the name Ryan. This might be deeper than he first thought. He began to panic; his position was exposed, and if he accepted the information that the youth offered, he would be neck deep in the thing, whatever it was.

"You're excused," said the PC, his voice rasping hoarsely. "Report to the chief inspector's office." He pressed the buzzer twice. The lieutenant appeared with dispatch.

Bill was going to try to plead his case further, but his pride grabbed hold of his tongue. He came to attention, saluted, did an about-face, and walked out. When he arrived in the hall, he was glad he hadn't said, "Thank you." He couldn't understand why the PC had frozen at the mention of his grandfather. It would be included in his report tonight.

After the cool reception by the PC, Bill was pleasantly surprised by the warmth of Chief Inspector Yates's greeting. "I understand," said Yates cordially, "that you're doing quite well in all phases of your training at the academy, Bill."

Bill flushed slightly, stunned but gratified that his work had somehow come to the attention of such a high official. It should have made him wary of the man, but with his youthful ego purposely inflated, he responded, "I'm doing my best, under the circumstances."

"Oh yes," said Yates. "The PC did allude to some problem that was troubling you." Bill proceeded to outline the events of the last two months, garnering an occasional "oh" or "really" from the intent chief inspector. Yates's feigned dismay turned to real disbelief when Bill handed him the notarized statement from the prisoner.

"What is it you want?" said Yates, measuring with newfound respect the young man seated alongside his desk.

"Our only interest is to get McGlick off my father's back," said Bill sincerely, "and to enable him to retire immediately."

"Did the clerk read this before he notarized it?" asked Yates in wonderment.

"No," said Bill, "I was afraid he wouldn't do it if he read it."

Yates smiled and shook his head in admiration. McGlick had been correct about this family; they were certainly resourceful. The grin vanished as Yates contemplated his predicament. He needed some answers.

"Do you have another copy of this?" asked Yates.

"I should have used a piece of carbon paper," Bill said, "but I was happy to get away with the original. I'll have to have it photocopied."

"I'll have that done," said Yates emphatically. "I'll need a few days to resolve this matter once and for all." Yates continued to probe.

"I guess the PC was as shocked as I was reading this?" asked Yates.

"No," said Bill, "he didn't want to see anything. He just referred me to you."

"Well, let me assure you," said Yates, "when he reads this, he's going to hit the ceiling. Let me handle this from here on out. In a few days, it will be a dead issue."

"I certainly hope so," said Bill. "This has been an excruciating period for my family. If you photocopy it, I'll take the original."

"That will take awhile," said Yates. "The machine is being serviced. Stop by tomorrow after your tour, and I'll give you back the original. Besides, I want the PC to see the original first. You can understand that, right?" Yates rose from his chair, put his arm around Bill's shoulders, and led him to the door. Yates's limp startled Bill, but at the same time reassured him; only a dedicated cop, considering Yates's age, would still suffer the police department with that affliction.

"By the way," said Bill, turning as he exited, "it might be nice if you could help that prisoner, Rodriguez, get off the hook too."

"Good point," said Yates. "I'll have someone take care of that too."

Bill made his report. Hugh and Grandpa picked up the mistakes, looking at each other on those occasions as Bill recounted his adventurous day. There was nothing that could be done to correct the errors now, so they kept silent on the blunders and glowingly praised the young man for his accomplishments. Grandpa knew their rear was unguarded; everything depended on whether or not Yates was involved in the headquarters part of the plot. Grandpa hoped that before their self-imposed forty-eight-hour limit expired, they would have the answer.

Later that night, Hector Rodriguez, loudly informed that he was being released on bail, was taken from his cell in the Bronx County Courthouse at 161st Street and transported in a private automobile to the Bronx House of Detention on River Avenue near Yankee Stadium, where he was lodged in the maximum-security area reserved for the most dangerous of the Bronx criminals under the name of Juan Rivera. Later, it would be excused as a regrettable but understandable bureaucratic blunder; the wrong man was let out on bail, the wrong man detained in jail.

32

IT WAS A COOL morning; Margaret had the oven on high with the door open to heat the room. A shawl over her shoulders, she drank her coffee and ate rye toast in the 6:00 AM solitude of her kitchen. It was her favorite time, a time of peace to listen undisturbed to the chirping wrens, to listen to herself, her innermost thoughts. She understood her men, and yet understanding them was not enough. Why couldn't they fathom her feelings and bend to her logic, which they both acknowledged was probably superior on the subject at hand? Why must they choose honor over adaptability, honor over life, especially when their foe wasn't the least bit honorable? Her men were a dying breed condemned by mental rather than physical Darwinism. A sense of tragedy pervaded her thoughts today.

The house was stirring at 7:00 AM when the phone rang. It was Captain Adler. He wanted to tell Hugh that although he was going to the pension section (the pressure of the constant transfers had been too much for him and his family) he would still testify on Hugh's behalf. The captain apologized for bailing out before the trial. Both men realized that his testimony would carry less weight now, coming from a civilian rather than an active member of the force. Hugh understood, perhaps too well. He thanked Adler for everything, especially for the kindness of the call. The tone of the day had been set.

Bill was waiting to be picked up by his recruit buddies. Today, they had to qualify on the speed chasing course at Jacob Riis Park in Brooklyn. Freddy Watts, a stocky, powerfully built black man, honked the horn of his beat-up Dodge. Bill ran out. The composition of the car pool reflected the changes that were taking place in the New York City Police Department.

Besides Watts, a thirty-three-year-old rookie with three children, there were Weiss, Ramos, and Cerbelli—a Jew, a Puerto Rican, and an Italian, respectively. The department was no longer the private preserve of the Irish. Watts would rise to detective sergeant, also managing to acquire a law degree on the way; Weiss would quit the department a disgruntled man five years later; Ramos would make detective third grade, only to be killed in a shootout two months before he could have retired; and Cerbelli would make lieutenant. These were the friends Bill made in the academy, and like in boot camp in the army, friends made there would remain his friends until the end.

As Watts's red Dodge pulled away from the house, Bill noticed the absence of the blue Ford sedan with Grandpa's ever-present shadow, Rogers. It disturbed Bill momentarily, but the ribbing had started and Bill's full wit was required to parry some sharp thrusts.

The number-one best-selling novel that summer had been *The Last Hurrah* by O'Conner. Grandpa, anticipating the favorable resolution of his son's case by Yates, sat in his favorite chair engrossed in the battles of the Irish politician Skeffington, hoping that the conniving bastard would somehow retain his throne but realizing that the title of the book presaged his eventual defeat.

Rogers' absence this morning hadn't upset Grandpa. In fact, it portended well for Hugh, he thought. It signaled to him a forced retreat on McGlick's part, another reason for hope.

Hugh, meanwhile, sat on the porch in his wicker rocker, reading *The Daily Mirror*. He had already decided not to report for duty tonight at midnight as directed, but would, on the advice of Dr. Cahill, report in sick again. The doctor assured him that he couldn't possibly be charged with malingering, as his electrocardiograms ruled that out.

It was a pleasant hour drive along the Belt Parkway for the five rookies before they reached the Riis Park training field, an empty parking lot transformed for three days into a speed chasing arena. Lieutenant Firestone, the course director, and his three instructors gathered the small class of fifteen on the grass alongside the field. While coffee and Danishes were served, Firestone, an erudite pipe smoker, lectured for a half-hour on the purpose of the course, the various skills to be acquired, and the rating system.

"If you do well in this course," he said, "you'll be assigned to chase speeders as members of the elite Special Traffic Enforcement Squad."

Cerbelli didn't care for the idea. "For four thousand dollars a year," he said, "I'm supposed to chase guys at 90 miles per hour to give them a ten-dollar ticket? It's ridiculous."

A slim officer standing nearby responded to Cerbelli's objection. "No, ya jerk, you pocket ten dollars and don't give him a ticket. What do you think this job is all about?" Bill and his small group moved away without comment.

Lieutenant Firestone had turned the class over to his top instructor, Don Chapman, a former stock car racer. "On this first exercise, you accelerate the vehicle to maximum speed," he said. "You should hit seventy-five, if you got guts. As you approach the cones out there, you should be coming in at about fifteen degrees. The cones are set up so there's a six-inch clearance on each side of the car. The purpose here is to test your perception and ability to pass slower vehicles as if you were in high-speed pursuit."

The second instructor, in RMP car number 1027 at the west end of the field, gunned his vehicle on Chapman's signal and executed the maneuver perfectly.

"Okay, Ryan, you missed yesterday, so you're first today," said the safety observer. "Use 728 over there." Bill moved enthusiastically to the car. As he clipped the safety belt around his waist, Lieutenant Firestone walked over to give him some final advice.

"Take the first run slowly," he said, "but on the next three runs, try to hit the maximum." Something was bothering Firestone as Ryan pulled away in 728, a 1955 Ford. He moved next to Chapman to make an inquiry. "Wasn't 728 involved in a front-end collision several months back?"

"Yeah," said Chapman, "we got it back from Motor Transport yesterday. They said it's in top shape."

Bill had started his first run, proceeding cautiously as directed, and passed through the cones at 50 miles per hour, without knocking any over. When Bill checked the rearview mirror, noting his accomplishment, his chest swelled with pride and confidence.

Firestone, suddenly horrified, saw the front left wheel wobbling savagely. Ryan had to be stopped. Firestone yelled to the visiting safety observer, who was several hundred feet away and the only person close enough to wave Ryan down. Later, the safety observer for the day, a sergeant from the Bronx named Rogers, moaned that he didn't hear the lieutenant's warning.

Ryan had reached maximum speed. He didn't see the frenzied abort signals of Firestone and Chapman.

As Bill sped through the cones, the vehicle suddenly swerved to the right, rocking violently, its tires screeching. Bill desperately, with all his strength, tried to turn the steering wheel to the left, but it was impossible. Only seconds before, brave and brazen, Bill was now instantly frightened, his ability to control his own fate gone.

It seemed like hours, but in milliseconds, all the good things in his life flashed in kaleidoscopic fashion before him. The car flipped over, crushed the roof on the passenger side, and slid one hundred feet to a grinding stop upside down. Bill, strapped in his seat, hung upside down, temporarily immobile. As he reached out to grab the door handle, a stream of blood cascaded, not unlike an open fire hydrant, from his right temple, and splattered his right arm with a constant stream of crimson. Blood also poured out his eyes and up his forehead into his hair. The thick liquid blinded him. Help arrived. He heard the voices. He was being unstrapped. Thank God, he thought, as he was lifted from the vehicle and laid on the concrete.

Freddy Watts had placed his police jacket under Bill's head. A passing motorist, a medic during the Korean War, had sped to the scene and was directing the efforts to stop the bleeding. Bill, semiconscious, felt pressure being applied to the top of his head and to the side of his face. Then the darkness came.

The police car had pulled up in front of the house, its siren still wailing softly, although turned off by Sergeant Norton as the cruiser screeched right from 233rd Street onto Dyre Avenue. Hugh and Margaret had gone to the door and looked at each other knowingly. In spite of Hugh's current problems, they both sensed that it was Bill. Grandpa dozed in his chair oblivious to the latest commotion. Hugh opened the door and walked down the fieldstone steps to meet the sergeant halfway. When their eyes met, Hugh said, "How bad is it?"

"The car turned over," said Sergeant Norton. "He should be at the hospital by now. I'll take you out."

Hugh cleared his throat. "Thanks," he said. "Give me a few minutes." Margaret called Bill's fiancée, Mary, at the telephone company on the Grand Concourse where she worked. They would pick her up.

Hugh took a deep breath, trying to regain the invisible life force that he believed each person possessed in measured amounts, some more than others, but quickly realized the futility of the act. He knew that you can only expend it; it isn't replenishable. When it has entirely vacated your body, as it eventually must, death follows swiftly.

Hugh nudged Grandpa gently, tenderly telling him of the accident in perhaps overly optimistic terms. Grandpa took it stoically externally, but his guts were churning. "Oh, dear Jesus," he cried to himself, "they did it; they actually did it." He silently agreed to watch the children while Hugh and Margaret rushed to pick up Mary and head for the hospital. When they were gone, Grandpa put his hands to his eyes and wept. The last time he had cried was in 1926. It had been for his wife. Today, he cried for the last time.

Grandpa would never discover if Skeffington overcame his political enemies for within five minutes, he, like Skeffington, a victim of the last hurrah, fell asleep for the final time in his favorite chair in the house he loved. It was a painless death, the kind of passing Grandpa had hoped that God would grant him. The children, noticing the slumbering giant, played quietly so as not to disturb their favorite storyteller.

After head x-rays, Bill was rushed into the operating room. Dr. Ernest Black, an honorary police surgeon passing the scene, responded to the hospital and took personal charge of the case. It was a five-hour, 211-stitch operation. Bill's right eye was sewn back in place. The exposed skull and severed temporal muscles were delicately repaired and the deep wound on the top of his head sutured. Bill, kept semiconscious by wads of cotton soaked in ammonia periodically stuffed into his nostrils, laughed at the irony of the nurse's repeated good-natured complaint as she injected each needle into his groggy head. On the way to the hospital, rushing to make her shift, she had received a speeding ticket from a member of the Special Traffic Enforcement Squad.

Margaret, Hugh, and Mary waited several hours before Bill was taken from surgery and placed in a ward. Margaret asked Mary to go in first, alone, afraid that the ghastly sight might shock Hugh into another heart attack. When Mary emerged, she said smiling, "He's fine; he's just wearing a turban and has two black eyes." The twin sighs could have turned a windmill. Mary had done her job well.

Hugh attributed Mary's observational deficiencies to her youth; his trained eye caught the deviated jaw unable to open, the right eye, and the swollen head. Bill wouldn't remember this visit for, without the constant ammonia treatment, he had drifted into a much-needed slumber. Dr. Black assured the parents that their son would survive and sent them home with orders not to return until tomorrow. Bill would sleep through the night.

Jack and Kathleen Faherty, sincerely concerned about their future son-in-law, welcomed the Ryans with great warmth and sympathy upon their arrival with Mary. A strong drink or two was needed, so Kathleen mixed and served lightly watered whiskeys.

The Fahertys had had some misgivings about the betrothal of their daughter to young Ryan. Bill, a high-spirited and good-natured lad, did have a bad temper. This worried Jack, whose family were peace-loving Galway fishermen. It was Kathleen, a Delaney by birth, brought up with three wild, hell-raising brothers, who finally prevailed. Kathleen recognized a certain goodness in the young man, which, if properly nurtured, would help him to transcend his insecurities and enable him to become a fine husband, father, and provider. She would never admit it, but in the sometimes difficult years that followed, Bill became her favorite son-in-law. To Jack, Bill would always remain a somewhat zany character, hiding his sentimentality and sincerity behind the mask of a jokester.

When Margaret called home to check on the kids, Kevin informed her that everything was fine, but that Grandpa was still dozing in his chair. It had been eight hours since they had left. Margaret became apprehensive; her woman's intuition told her that the worst had happened.

Margaret briefly explained her fears to Hugh and the Fahertys. They left abruptly. Sergeant Norton, with siren blaring, drove them home in silence. Margaret and Hugh rushed into the house with Norton right behind them. Margaret herded the lads upstairs while Hugh and Norton vainly groped for signs of life. "Rigor mortis," whispered Norton.

"Oh, my God," said Hugh, sliding backward into his armchair. "This was just one too many for him."

Margaret, in a daze, slowly descended the stairs, drifted toward Hugh's chair, and sat down on the arm, wrapping her right hand around Hugh's neck. By now, Hugh was reflecting on the incredible man, his father, who lay dead before him.

"I honestly thought he was indestructible," said Hugh, his eyes filling with moisture. "He must have died shortly after we left." Hugh looked at Margaret. Silent tears were dropping from her chin. She fell, crying softly, into his gentle embrace. Norton, a veteran sergeant, had been shaken by the unprecedented events of the day. He called the precinct for assistance. This was one tour he would never forget.

＊　＊　＊

Rogers sat trembling and sobbing on McGlick's office couch. McGlick patted him on the shoulder. "Relax, Sarge," he said, "the kid will live—I've checked." Rogers blew his nose. I can't use this bastard anymore, thought McGlick. He'd fall apart on me if things really got tough. A good DA would have him spilling his fuckin' guts.

"You better take the rest of the day off," he told Rogers. "This has been a terrible day—I have to help that poor family," McGlick added for Rogers' benefit. He buzzed his clerical lieutenant. Rogers was wiping his eyes.

"Lieutenant," said McGlick, as the man entered, "get a car to take the sergeant home." McGlick told the lieutenant with his eyes and head gestures to get Rogers the hell out of his office. The lieutenant moved swiftly.

After they had left, McGlick smiled. God is on my side, he mused. Rogers was supposed to let the kid see him. Then, when the kid reported to his grandfather that Rogers was at the training course, the old man would know that the stakes in this battle had been raised. If that didn't spook the old bastard, nothing would, McGlick had figured. Now, thought McGlick, with the accident, the old man will really be distraught. McGlick was elated. He couldn't wait to find out how the old man had reacted.

Later that night, he heard; the old man had died. McGlick's sense of power reached dizzying heights. The thrill of this victory surpassed anything he had ever felt before; even his Olympic win paled in comparison. Even his greatest sexual conquest, the senator's wife, was nothing now. He had, in his own mind, reached the pinnacle in human power: the control of life and death. For him, it was the ultimate orgasm.

MOST EX-POLICEMEN were buried out of a Walter B. Cooke funeral home; old Walter not only liked cops, but also provided a decent discount. The Ryans appreciated Cooke's kind gesture of respect, the significance of which wasn't lost on active officers either, but Grandpa had made his own arrangements. Mullarky and O'Rorke, originally located in the Irish ghetto parish of Saint Luke's in the South Bronx, had picked up their old friend and taken him to their Castle Hill Avenue parlor. They spent the night preparing Grandpa for viewing at 2:00 PM the next day.

Hugh, excused from duty for three days because of his father's death—it was in the union contract—had spent a difficult night. The loss of his father was distressing enough, but to lose a man who, in addition, shared your love for fishing, horse racing, and baseball, who acted as your advisor and tactician, and whose presence in your home delighted your wife, children, and guests, was devastating. Margaret had also spent a sleepless night, trying to soothe and comfort her distraught husband while her own anguish switched focus back and forth between Grandpa and Bill. About 5:00 AM, they had given up their bed for the kitchen where they sat solemnly, sipping cup after cup of coffee.

It was a few minutes after eight. Margaret was now dozing on the couch; she would miss the eight o'clock Mass. Hugh struggled with his emotions in the kitchen, smoking a Pall Mall over another cup of coffee. The doorbell rang twice. He recognized the figure at the door; it was

Sergeant Norton. Hugh welcomed the sergeant and led him into the kitchen where he insisted that he share the pot of coffee.

"I appreciate you stopping by," said Hugh. "It's been a rough night." Sergeant Norton was fidgety and ill at ease.

"I know," said Norton, commiserating with Hugh. "You've really had a bad time of it." Norton looked away as he removed some folded papers from his police blouse pocket and handed them to Hugh. "It's routine," said Norton. "Just a notification. The department's timing is atrocious though—makes you wonder sometimes."

Hugh unfolded the two sheets of paper. Norton was right. It was routine; his trial had been set for September 7, just two days away. Hugh signed the second sheet and returned the carbon to Norton.

"I checked with the union and headquarters," said Norton. "We figured that your three-day death-in-the-family leave should have included the seventh, but we were told it started on the day your father died, the fourth."

"Thanks, Norton," said Hugh. "At least you spared me that aggravation."

A troubled Norton walked down the front steps to his marked police car. Today, he had a chauffeur. Yesterday, as the extra sergeant, he had volunteered to drive the Ryans to the hospital rather than break up a radio car team.

"How did he take it?" the chauffeur wanted to know.

"Yeah, okay," said Norton, his mind sifting through the intonations, connotations, and attitudes of those he had called this morning to get a ruling on Ryan. "You know," he said after a significant delay, "if I didn't know better, I'd swear that they were trying to kill this guy—"

"And his family too?"

"You're probably right," said Norton, picking up the chauffeur's meaning. "It does sound incredible," he added, agreeing with the cop. "But I just can't shake that feeling."

Mullarky and O'Rorke had honored their dead friend's wishes: a minimum of cutting, no stuffing, and most importantly, making sure that the ankle high shoes were on his feet. To accomplish the latter wish, O'Rorke had spent nearly two hours cutting and re-sewing the shoes while adjusting the fit. Both men laughed frequently while making the arrangements; this was going to be a fun funeral.

Father O'Hara had stopped by the house to discuss his eulogy and the funeral arrangements. Margaret sat with him in the dining room while the children romped in the living room. In later years, each child would remember fondly those special moments and stories that their grandfather had shared with them, though his death had no special meaning now; Grandpa was just taking a long nap. Hugh, responding from the second floor to Margaret's call that the priest had arrived, shushed the kids as he passed into the dining area.

Hugh had been in his upstairs den sifting through Grandpa's insurance policies and other papers. While doing that, he also made sure that his own will and documents were in order. It hadn't taken much effort or time, thus giving Hugh some needed moments to reflect on the Ryan summer. The mental summation produced one outstanding image: fuckin' disaster. After yesterday, nothing could shock him. Sergeant Norton's visit this morning, no doubt meant by certain individuals to unnerve him further, had had the opposite effect. When he surprisingly discovered that he was inured to that ploy, his attitude became more aggressive. They had indirectly killed his father and possibly maimed his son. He was the only one left to hurt. When Margaret called, he had decided that he would go to his death fighting, spitting in their eyes. He owed it to his father and son.

After Father O'Hara left, Hugh told Margaret of his decision; he could not now quit with honor and self-respect. It could be no other way; he had been pushed too far. He had to do battle. Naturally upset, Margaret knew that there would be no changing his mind now. She kissed him gently. "Whatever you do, dear," she said, "you have my complete support."

That afternoon, Margaret and Hugh rode by cab to Mullarky and O'Rorke's to visit with Grandpa. True to their word, the undertakers had carried out all of Grandpa's wishes; he looked absolutely terrible in his coffin.

As the visitors entered, they were handed a card entitling them to a free drink at Cafferty's Cafe, further down on the avenue near the firehouse. As those paying their respects knelt to pray before the unimpressive corpse, another card was slapped into their hand by Mullarky. It read, "What the hell did you expect?" Some just shook their heads. Others laughed. A few more were shocked. When the users of the first card—and most did use it—arrived at Cafferty's Cafe and gave the card to the proprietor, they were handed yet another card which read, "Fuck you, dead men don't buy." It caused many a good-natured laugh and slap on the back. It was something that Grandpa had enjoyed immensely in life, putting people on, and he saw no reason to stop now that he was dead. Grandpa had been to many funerals. The one remark that had constantly infuriated him was the ridiculous, "Oh my, he really looks good." No one would say that at this wake.

"Grandpa was unique," said Hugh to a grinning Mullarky.

With a twinkle in his eye, Mullarky replied, "There will never be another like him." It turned out to be the best wake in years.

Bill had, on the night of the third, stopped at the Rodriguez home, as he was asked to do by Hector, and told the man's wife of his improper arrest. Bill had given the woman his telephone number, asking to be apprised of the disposition of the case. Carmen Rodriguez went to the courthouse the next morning to make inquiries as to the whereabouts of her husband. To her relief, she was told that Hector had been freed on bail. But Hector wasn't at home or at work. Her concern for his safety grew as the hours passed and he failed to appear. When she called Bill at his home this afternoon and heard about the accident, she worried more. She didn't know where to turn. In panic, she went to the Three-nine Precinct and reported her husband missing.

Hector Rodriguez, logged in at the detention center as Juan Rivera, had spent two edgy and distressing nights wondering why his wife and family had abandoned him. The Puerto Rican prisoner in the next cell had tried to console Hector, weathering several of his hysterical outbursts. The sympathetic prisoner had listened with interest to Hector's tale of the strange chain of events which led to the maximum-security cellblock. The other prisoner assured Rodriguez that an error must have been made and spoke to a friendly corrections officer who agreed to look into the matter.

Dr. Black reluctantly agreed to allow Bill to attend the funeral, though it would have to be in a wheelchair; there was still the possibility of future complications. Although the present prognosis was good, constant monitoring was prescribed.

Tears had come to Bill's eyes when told of Grandpa's peaceful death. He loved the old man for many reasons: his caring wisdom, his blunt honesty, and especially, his off-center wit, which reflected the traditional flaky Irish approach to reality. But the tears dried quickly; it was impossible to feel sorry for a man who had lived such a long, rich life. It was Bill who started the "remember the time ritual" as Hugh and Margaret sat red-eyed at his bedside, nodding.

34

GRANDPA HAD DECREED an early low Mass, a quick burial, and then the customary grand celebration lasting well into the night. His orders were obeyed. Father O'Hara streaked through the Mass in twenty-four minutes; the cortege sped to the family plot in the Gate of Heaven Cemetery in Valhalla, New York, in twenty-three minutes; the burial service took seven minutes, and then the shiny black procession rushed to the Red Rooster Restaurant in Pleasantville, which took another five minutes. Fifty-nine minutes—it was a family record, a parish record, and maybe even a world record for Catholic internments.

Everyone had a drink in hand before the hour was up, toasting Grandpa on his last victory. Things slowed down now. There was serious business afoot. Each guest present was required to tell either a funny story about the deceased or a personal remembrance or say a prayer.

It struck invited outsiders as strange to hear these obviously reverent Catholics being so irreverent toward their recently departed and beloved grandfather, father, and friend, but it was their way, the only way Grandpa would have had it. After the luncheon, all serious partiers, including Mullarky, O'Rorke, and Father O'Hara, would return to the big house in the Bronx to eat, drink, talk, and sing into the wee hours for today was for celebration.

Bill, in his wheelchair and still wearing his white turban over two black eyes, was dumped into the back of the hearse by Mullarky and O'Rorke for the ride home. The two undertakers, already half drunk, had one last chore to perform for their buddy of fifty years.

The hearse, with a confused Bill rolling back and forth in the rear, zigzagged erratically back to the cemetery, screeching to a halt before the recently filled grave. Mullarky and O'Rorke solemnly walked to the gravesite and calmly relieved their bladders into the churned-up clay. They shook themselves vigorously and while laughing wildly, stumbled, unable to retrieve their zippers, back to the hearse and sped south with their passenger rollicking with laughter in the rear.

The sacred and the profane, each revolving spheres, occasionally touch each other. One's interpretation of this touching depends upon which globe one is sitting in at the time of contact. The three men agreed that this outrageously obscene act was in reality an act of love. Grandpa, hopefully viewing it from the upper spirit world, would have concurred, but the groundskeepers and a nearby funeral procession didn't.

The speeding hearse was stopped in Greenberg, New York, by an alerted town cop who issued a summons to the two men for urinating in public while, as he later recalled, some pervert in a wheelchair laughed himself hoarse in the rear. And the party hadn't even started yet.

✼ ✼ ✼

Brown and Bubba were in Smalls on Lennox Avenue enjoying Jack Daniel sour mashes when Elijah peered in the window, saw them, and entered. "Uncle Tom's bank is hanging, baby," said Elijah, smacking the palms of his hands into Bubba's.

"Okay, man, then let's do it," said Bubba, exposing his uneven teeth in a grin. Brown and Elijah strutted to the blue Cadillac.

It was a short drive to their Amsterdam Avenue armory, adjacent to the City College of New York, where they secured two machine guns, one sawed-off shotgun, one .357 Magnum, and one military police .45-caliber automatic. It had all been prearranged; all they needed was the location. Elijah had gotten that tonight from a paid informer—his price, heroin.

The five men gathered in Bubba's basement pad on 147th Street in a well-kept brownstone on a block of similar homes. It was called the street without numbers. There were no house addresses, as all the street's inhabitants were in various nefarious occupations, and it was to their advantage that neither the law nor the Mafia could readily contact them.

Brown laid out their tactics after Elijah drew a map showing where the metal doors were located, the sentry placed, and the money room situated. Since Brown had once worked in a numbers bank, he was able to brief his men on the expected response to their attack by the bank personnel. Their informer had given them some critical information.

Tonight, as they did every Tuesday night, Uncle Tom and his top lieutenants paid a visit to Madam LaVerne's to try out her latest acquisitions. The word on the street was that the madam had hired at least five new girls, which meant that Uncle Tom had a full night ahead of him. Brown and Bubba were certain that it would be easy pickings.

"If things go well tonight," said Brown impishly, "maybe we can all pay Madam LaVerne a visit."

A chorus of "indeeds" greeted his suggestion.

Bubba placed two sticks of dynamite by the hinges of the steel door, lit the fuse, and ran. The resulting explosion not only ripped out the door, but left gaping holes in both the ceiling and floor. A voice could be heard yelling from above, "Hey, baby, tell those mothers downstairs to go light on the drums."

Elijah, Bubba, and Brown leaped over the hole in the floor and stormed the money room. It was empty. Brown was uneasy; the expected assault from the rear hadn't materialized. Scooping the few thousand dollars on the counting table, they hustled back out the front door.

As they raced from the brownstone and down the stairs, Captain Stevens shouted, "Fire!" The roar from the machine guns was deafening. Bubba and Elijah were ripped apart by the .45-caliber bullets. One police officer fell wounded as Brown fired one blast from his sawed-off shotgun before he, too, was riddled by dumdum bullets and collapsed dead onto the sidewalk. The two backup men had been silently captured earlier, after the gang had entered the building.

The stakeout had worked to perfection. Debts had been paid; peace had been secured. Uncle Tom's reputation was strengthened and Captain Stevens's earlier blunder redeemed, making him once again eligible for promotion. A cop had lost the use of his right arm, but that didn't overly concern the police power brokers involved in this setup as, after all, cops got 4,000 dollars a year to run those risks.

※　※　※

It was nearly midnight. The Ryans and their guests were still going strong, burying their loss in the traditional Irish way: drink, song, and laughter. Mullarky had his arm around Hugh; both swayed side to side.

"I think I was wrong," said Mullarky.

"About what?" asked Hugh. They were shouting now, the house echoed with strains of "Kilcullen's Lament," commonly known as "Danny Boy."

"About not seeing the likes of your father again," yelled Mullarky. "I think that boy of yours is just as goofy."

"That's what I'm worried about," screamed Hugh, a chuckle in his voice. "Which son do you mean?"

Both men took a swig of Irish whiskey and joined the chorus singing a song about a father's love for his son and his hope that that love would be returned.

The summer's gone and all the flowers are dying.
And I am dead, as dead I well may be.
You'll come and find the place where I am lying,
And kneel and say an Ave there for me.
And I shall hear, though soft you tread above me,
For you will kneel and tell me that you love me.
And I shall sleep in peace until you come to me.

COMATOSE BODIES WERE everywhere Margaret looked—on the couch, on the floor, on the porch. When she went outside to retrieve the milk and *Daily News*, which headlined Brown's and Bubba's demises in Harlem last night, she saw two more prone silhouettes in the ivy under the pine trees. She felt good. It had been a wake befitting an Irish lord, and Grandpa was certainly that. After putting on two pots of coffee, she went upstairs to rouse Hugh; today his trial began.

Bill hadn't slept all night—at least he didn't think he had. His head hurt, but he couldn't be sure why. He staggered downstairs and joined his mother and father in the kitchen. If his father was going on trial, he was going with him. Hugh was touched by the gesture and decided over Margaret's objections to let his son do as he saw fit. In a sense, it was a reconciliation for the two men.

On occasion, Hugh had been severe in the treatment of his son; he hadn't spared the rod and hoped that someday Bill would see it as a sign of caring. Bill recognized that he had been a disciplinary problem but still couldn't fully understand why. In later years, he would finally resolve the love-hate relationship and realize that his father was motivated by love. But for now, it was enough to know that his father needed him.

Uncle Fred volunteered to drive them to the headquarters trial room. Fred, who was not in much better shape than his passengers, couldn't start his car; he had left the headlights on overnight, and the battery was dead. Since Mullarky and O'Rorke's hearse was the first of ten cars parked in the long, clogged driveway, and as both morticians still snored contently under the pines, Fred gingerly took O'Rorke's keys, and the three suddenly non-superstitious, hung-over men headed for the tribunal in the black hearse.

The symbolism of their arrival wasn't lost on several chiefs and inspectors who watched Ryan and his son alight from the hearse directly in front of headquarters. Word of their unusual arrival spread rapidly through the building; the lower ranks enjoyed the humor and daring of the apparently masochistic Ryans, while the upper echelons viewed it as yet another sign of Ryan's defiance and contempt for the system, a good enough reason for harsh treatment.

Fred had parked the vehicle, stretched out in the rear, and nodded off immediately. Bill, who had abandoned the wheelchair last night, and Hugh, both tight-lipped, sucking on rum-flavored Life Savers, took the crowded elevator to the third-floor trial room.

It was no surprise to Hugh; he nudged his son, directing Bill's glance toward the far corner where the defense attorney was engaged in a friendly conversation with his adversary, McGlick.

"He's working out a deal for me," said Hugh sarcastically.

"Yeah, ten years in Brooklyn," said Bill.

Seeing the Ryans, Kahn casually broke off from McGlick and ambled over to them. "Sorry to hear about your accident," he said. Kahn didn't wait for a reply. "That business with the hearse was in poor taste, Hugh. It got everyone upset."

"Who's everyone?" said Hugh coldly.

"You know what I mean," said Kahn.

Hugh was in no mood to placate anyone. "Well, it's tough, Counselor," he said. "I'll ride in anything I want to. So I've hurt their sensibilities? Look at my son. And I buried a father yesterday." Hugh's voice was rising.

"Take it easy," said the lawyer anxiously.

"I don't give a damn who hears me," said Hugh, staring across the room at the scowling McGlick.

"Dad," said Bill, "forget that creep. Let's get down to business." The lawyer led them to the defense table.

Hugh was still fuming. "Did Yates send you a copy of the prisoner's notarized statement?" he asked. Kahn's blank stare caused Hugh to add,

"About the unprovoked attack on the prisoner by McGlick. It happened on September 3."

"I spoke to the chief inspector on this case this morning," said Kahn, frowning. "He said nothing about a notarized statement from a prisoner; in fact, what he did say was that he was pushing for the maximum penalty in this case. Do you have a duplicate copy?"

Bill was completely sober now. He hadn't attempted to get the duplicate because of his accident. He understood his father's smirk.

"It's all right, son," said Hugh. "You did your best. It's kind of late, but we finally found out who's backing McGlick: Yates."

The lawyer didn't believe the story that followed. "If what you say is true," said Kahn, challenging the veracity of the two men, "why don't we subpoena the prisoner?"

Hugh handed a pad and pencil to Bill. The young man wrote out all the information that he had on the prisoner. Kahn handed the paper to his assistant and told him to check it out.

The department judge, in this case a lawyer-lieutenant, had his arrival announced by the court clerk, a law student-cop. Everyone stood, except Bill. "I only stand up for God, the flag, and honest judges," whispered Bill defiantly to Kahn.

"You have to play the game by the rules, kid," said Kahn, "even when you're losing. It's still the only game in town. Why get the umpire mad at you?"

Bill realized that Kahn was right, but his sense of justice had, only moments before, been shattered once again by Yates, and anyway, he didn't feel like honoring anyone right now. The judge was staring at him. Kahn pointed to the bandage around the young man's head; the judge acknowledged with a nod.

"Don't assume that everyone's your enemy," whispered Kahn earnestly. "It's poor tactics. I'm sure your father would agree."

Hugh knew that Kahn was correct, but he wasn't about to go against his son now. He grinned and winked at Bill.

The judge gaveled the court to order, read the charges against the accused, and asked for Ryan's plea. Hugh stood and in a loud, unwavering voice said, "Not guilty."

McGlick sneered.

"Is the prosecution ready?" asked the judge.

"Yes, Your Honor," said the department prosecutor.

"Is the defense ready?" asked the judge.

"May I approach the bench, Your Honor?" requested Kahn. The judge waved him forward.

Kahn told the judge that some new evidence that might lend credence to his client's case was being investigated and that in the interest of fairness, a postponement was in order.

McGlick fidgeted angrily in his seat, trying to catch the judge's eye to register his displeasure at what he suspected was taking place. At McGlick's prodding, the prosecutor approached the bench and vehemently registered his objection.

While this discussion was proceeding, Kahn's assistant reentered the courtroom and approached the small group at the bench.

"There was a bureaucratic mix-up," said the keyed-up assistant. "Hector Rodriguez was erroneously sent to the Bronx House of Detention under the wrong name instead of being released on bail." He hesitated before dropping the bomb. "The guy committed suicide last night."

Kahn was stunned. He nervously pleaded for an adjournment. When the judge asked him what the significance of the suicide was, Kahn sidestepped the question, as he feared committing himself to the serious allegations Ryan had made against Yates.

"I'm not quite sure, Your Honor," Kahn said, "but I think the prosecutor would agree to setting a new date on this now." Kahn emphasized the "now."

The prosecutor, having worked with Kahn for several years, understood that Kahn was in a tight spot and agreed to the adjournment. Later, the prosecutor would have to listen to a twenty-minute tirade from McGlick and be forced to apologize to the inspector by his superior for making the supposed tactical error. Anyway, thought the prosecutor, a little humiliation is better than going back to patrol.

Kahn now believed Ryan's story. But believing it was one thing; proving it would be nearly impossible. And even if he could substantiate the allegations, would he want to try? Those famous horns: his moral-legal convictions versus his career aspirations—he wouldn't be the last to face that dilemma, and he wouldn't be the last to choose his career. If Ryan could prove his case, more power to him, Kahn concluded, but he wasn't getting involved in this case outside the trial room.

During the ride home, Bill stared out the hearse window at the barges and tugs working in the East River where other Irishmen toiled. Bill's sorrow, increased by the gentle Rodriguez's suicide, made him wonder if a life on the river would have been more pleasant for the Ryans. It seemed so peaceful out there.

Nothing had changed, Hugh realized; he was still fodder for McGlick's gun, waiting for the trigger to be pulled. The ploys, attacks, maneuvers, deaths, and delays had literally torn him apart. He was sorry that a final disposition hadn't been reached today. He could live with any decision, but the continuous holding out of false hope, well, that was killing him.

✷ ✷ ✷

Bill answered the phone. It was Dutch Van Buren again. Dutch wanted to know the outcome of Hugh's trial room appearance. Bill sensed that Van Buren was looking for information, holding back while picking his brain before committing himself to any course of action.

Bill openly discussed with Dutch his suspicions concerning the Yates-McGlick conspiracy, the police commissioner's reluctance to get involved, the fear he observed in the defense attorney's eyes, the notarized statement, and the death of the prisoner, Rodriguez.

"I guess there's nobody who could help your father," said Dutch, "even if you had some evidence."

"Well, it's not encouraging," said Bill, "but if we had to do it all over again, we would go to the Manhattan district attorney, Hogan." There was a pause.

"Yeah, well, I have to go to court tomorrow," said Van Buren casually. "Can you meet me about 1:00 PM at the Three-nine Precinct?"

"Sure, I'll be there," said Bill, somewhat confused as to the need for such a meeting. Van Buren hung up.

"Who was that?" said Hugh, sitting in his rocking chair, sucking on a licorice stick while watching television.

"Just a friend," said Bill, "just a friend." No more false hopes.

36

AN EXHAUSTED Van Buren greeted Bill in front of the precinct station house. "I've been waiting," said Dutch. "It's been a tough day. Let's take my car."

Bill was looking for some answers. "Where are we going?" he asked.

"I want you to meet some people," said Van Buren. "Relax, this might help."

Dutch maneuvered his Volkswagen in and out of traffic skillfully for twenty minutes before they reached their destination, the Old Homestead on Ninth Avenue at Thirteenth Street, a restaurant noted for its steak.

Van Buren and Bill were ushered into a private dining area where three grim, though distinguished-looking, gentlemen sat robustly eating. "Sit down," said the man in the black pinstriped suit. "Take their order, Charlie."

Bill recognized the two other men; he nervously ordered a whiskey.

"Dutch," said the same man, "I think it's time that you told Bill what happened yesterday."

"Well, yesterday," said Dutch, "I went to the Bronx House of Detention to pick up a rape suspect, Raoul Guzman, to bring him to another lineup at the DA's office. He was very upset. The guy in the next cell, a guy named Rodriguez, had committed suicide the night before. On the way to the Grand Concourse, this Raoul tells me about the guy in the next cell—the guy's story about being beat up by this crazy

185

Inspector McGlick while inside the Three-nine Precinct, about a guy writing down his story, about the late-night transfer to River Avenue.

"Naturally, I knew about the beating. The entire division did; it was McGlick again. It didn't prove anything, so I forgot it. Well, we go to the DA's office, and two more women pick out Guzman as the rapist. It's all over, so I'm taking him back to the prison. All of a sudden, this Raoul says to me, 'That must have been the same guy I saw on 138th Street, fighting with the sergeant.' Now that struck home. So I asked him what he saw. He told me that he had been out searching for a victim when he heard police sirens on the street below and ducked down. A few minutes later, he heard the shattering of glass and instinctively looked over the roof ledge. He said that a sergeant and another big guy had crashed through the bar window and were rolling in the street. He figured that the big guy was a boss because when he got up he yelled, 'Insubordination,' a few times and then left.

"Well, after I talked to you last night, Bill, I called Mr. Hogan here," continued Van Buren, pointing to the Manhattan district attorney.

"Whew," was the best Bill could manage.

"In case you didn't recognize them," said Mr. Hogan, "this is the police commissioner, and this is Chief Inspector Yates."

"Yes," said Bill, "I've met them both before."

"Both agree," said the dapper Hogan, "that a horrible error has been made and they would like to correct it. I understand that your father is quite ill and that you just buried your grandfather, so I felt it was best if we contacted you instead of your father. This offer is a compromise solution, subject, of course, to your father's approval." Yates and the PC continued eating as if unconcerned with the conversation.

"That's fine, Mr. Hogan," said Bill. "What's the deal?"

"Your father's application for a medical discharge will be granted," said Hogan, with compassion. "Whether it's line-of-duty or ordinary medical retirement is up to the medical board." He hesitated while he studied the young man's face. "But the main thing is that charges against your father will be dropped, technically filed with no disposition, and he will be able to retire immediately. How's that?"

Although Bill tried not to show it, it was evident that he was elated. He wanted to jump up and yell with delight. Somehow, he temporarily resisted the urge. "That sounds fair, sir," was all he said.

"All your father has to do," said Hogan, "is to call the PC's office later today or tomorrow with his decision. He will be retired the following day; one day is needed to get the medical board's decision."

The food had arrived, but Bill wanted to get home to share the good news; he was bursting. Dutch understood. Bill extended his right hand to Hogan. "Thank you, Mister District Attorney," he said with all the sincerity he could muster. The Manhattan DA's firm handshake, blue-grey gaze, and faint smile assured Bill that his optimism was on solid ground.

Once outside, Bill embraced Van Buren warmly then jumped into the air, throwing his right arm skyward, and yelled, "Whoopee!" Then the two young men grasped each other firmly once again and headed for the car.

Van Buren was more talkative on the return trip. He explained to Bill why he was interested in helping anyone who had been abused by McGlick. The story left Bill shaking his head. "I believe it. I believe it," a happy Bill kept saying. Dutch then shared some of his good fortune.

"This morning, I was assured of a gold shield," said Dutch, "for my part in the capture of the rapist."

When Bill started to laugh, Dutch quickly joined him. Both men were well aware of what was being rewarded; it was Van Buren's silence on the Ryan affair. It was ironic, but McGlick had made Dutch a detective. They laughed at that too.

The good cheer ended upon their arrival at the Three-nine Precinct station house. McGlick was waiting near Bill's car to make sure he didn't miss the young officer. Van Buren, with much trepidation, stood a few yards away as Bill walked brazenly toward his car and McGlick.

"You won this one, Ryan," said McGlick fiercely, "but sooner or later, I'll get you."

"You probably will," said Bill, smiling, "but it's not going to be easy, baby. Your kind has seen their last day in this department."

"Listen, punk," said McGlick, "my kind always gets to the top on this job." McGlick was getting hot.

"Well," said Bill, sliding into his car and rolling down the window, "as far as I'm concerned, your type are nothing but a bunch of assassins."

Bill quickly rolled up the window and drove off, leaving McGlick cursing him in the street. Bill could feel himself shaking. That guy is a bad, bad bastard, he thought. After a few blocks, he smiled, thinking that it took a special kind of man to go head to head with McGlick, and his father had. He was never prouder to be his father's son than at that moment. It was ironic, but McGlick had made him see it.

"I've got some good news," said Bill, bubbling enthusiastically as he ran into the kitchen. The family had just sat down for an early baked macaroni dinner.

"Can't it wait until after supper?" asked Margaret firmly.

"No way," said Bill. "We won! They're giving Dad his medical pension, no trial, no nothing." It didn't register.

"It's just another ploy, Bill," said Hugh calmly. "After yesterday, I'm sure of it."

"You didn't hear about last night, though, Dad," said Bill, raising his voice. "Van Buren went to Hogan. Hogan put the pressure on them."

"Wait a minute," said Hugh. "Margaret, serve the children and then join us in the living room."

It took Bill less than five minutes to explain the fortuitous and welcome developments—at least Hugh was smiling, though he couldn't manage anything more yet. He went immediately to the telephone and dialed police headquarters.

"PC's office," he said. His face had tensed and drained to white. "It's Sergeant Ryan." There was a pause. "Yes, Commissioner," said Hugh. Another pause.

Bill and Margaret waited anxiously through the second, seemingly eternal pause. The commissioner must be explaining the terms of the deal, Bill correctly figured.

Finally, Hugh said, "I can accept those terms, sir, but what are my chances of getting the three-quarters pension? The heart attack did occur on the job." Again, there was a long pause. "I understand," said Hugh. "Right. Thank you, Commissioner."

A good soldier to the end, thought Bill.

Hugh hung up. He smiled emotionally at Margaret.

"It's over," he said, a tear fighting its way out of his left eye. Hugh had suppressed his emotions for too long.

Margaret rushed to embrace him, to share his relief, to share the mixed feelings of joy and sadness. It was a victory. The war had been won, but the casualties had been heavy—perhaps too heavy. But for the moment, happiness prevailed. It was over. That was the most important thing.

The battles were over, at least for Hugh, and for that, a small celebration was required. It wouldn't be the same without Grandpa. They all knew that. But although physically absent, Grandpa's warm spirit filled the big, and once again, happy house. The good news had arrived just in the nick of time, for tomorrow was Bill's graduation from the police academy, traditionally a day of fun and festivity in the Ryan family. And so it would be once more.

37

THE RYAN FAMILY was well represented at the 11:00 AM ceremony, fourteen in all. They had their own cheering section. Bill attended with Dr. Cahill's approval, his head still bandaged, his eyes black. "If he survived the wake," the doctor said, "there's no reason for him to miss a simple graduation."

The cast of dignitaries on the stage was outstanding: the lieutenant governor, the junior senator, the attorney general, the mayor, and the police commissioner. But the most impressive personage present was Bishop Sheen, the most popular Catholic in New York and possibly in the country. The bishop gave a stirring benediction; the applause deafened ears, tingled spines, and annoyed the hell out of the mayor, who followed the bishop to the podium. The mayor's speech received polite applause from the audience, though those on the stage gave him a standing ovation. The mayor stared intently at the police commissioner as he returned to his seat. The message was received.

The police commissioner was next. The class, on cue, jumped to attention en masse. "Be seated," the commissioner said. Once again, the entire class moved as one. "I would like to take this opportunity to announce," the PC said, without much verve, "several changes and promotions that have been made earlier this morning. I think that this is a most appropriate and proper occasion for such announcements, as they demonstrate to our graduating officers that honesty, dedication, and hard work are rewarded." There was a sprinkling of applause. "First, with deep regret and sorrow, I have accepted Chief Yates's resignation because of health reasons. He has been an inspiration to all of us. May he enjoy his retirement." Respectful applause followed. Yates stood up and took a bow.

"My choice for the new chief inspector was a difficult one," the PC continued, "but I have made an unusual move, reaching deep into our reservoir of talent and promoting Inspector Terence McGlick to that post." The boos from the Ryan cheering section on the left side of the auditorium were clearly heard. Hugh just looked at Margaret and frowned in disgust. Yates had pulled it off for McGlick with some expensive help from Kimble, the mayor's aide. He had to; McGlick was furious, threatening reprisals when DA Hogan extricated Ryan from the hook. It cost Yates another five grand, but it was worth it. McGlick had been diffused, appeased with the offer of increased power.

Included in the promotions were Chief Crown from the Bronx and Dutch Van Buren from the Three-nine Precinct. The latter announcement was greeted with wild cheers from the left side of the auditorium. The new chief inspector was then called upon by the police commissioner to hand out the awards to the outstanding rookies in the several categories.

The first two awards, off-duty revolvers, were presented to the best marksman in the class and the best athlete in the physical school. The third award, the Bloomingdale Trophy, was to be presented to the officer with the highest academic average.

"The winner of the academic award, the Bloomingdale Trophy," said McGlick, "is Bill Ryan." Shouts of elation sprang from the left side of the hall. McGlick then realized just who that was. Hugh had instantly recovered from his revulsion with McGlick's promotion and was suddenly deliriously happy. Bill, completely surprised, as all awards were held top secret, bashfully strolled toward the stage. McGlick was scowling on the stage, outraged that he had to present the award.

It wasn't until Bill reached the stage that he too fully comprehended the situation; his self-effacing smile had turned to a cool stare. It was an unpleasant and distasteful chore for both men. McGlick handed Bill the trophy and turned away, neither verbally acknowledging Bill's feat nor extending his hand to congratulate the young man. The audience gasped at the obviously rude gesture. Police Commissioner O'Grady smiled at the mayor; they were even. O'Grady had been against McGlick's elevation, but the mayor had listened to his man, Kimble. Now, the mayor made another decision. He would stick with McGlick until he made his next mistake, which, he was sure, wouldn't take too long.

Bill spoke into the microphone. "I'd like to dedicate this trophy to my father, mother, and grandfather," he said. "I'd also like to thank the new chief inspector for the gracious manner in which he presented it." The audience, especially the recruits, and some dignitaries on the dais loudly applauded the spunk of the young recipient.

That afternoon at three, Hugh received the phone call from the medical unit informing him that the medical board had voted him ordinary disability on the basis that his heart attack wasn't job related. It hurt him financially, and even though he had expected that decision, he was still disappointed. He consoled himself with the thought that at least he was alive and free.

The party had been a good one. At midnight, Hugh went to the hall closet and removed his nightstick from the coat hook where it hung by the thong. Going into the living room, he yelled, "Attention, attention, everyone!" Hugh proposed a toast. He was now officially retired. "To life and freedom, to God and the law … to Grandpa." He slapped the stick into Bill's hand, as Bill had requested he do back—it seemed like years ago—on July 6. Everyone cheered, gulped his drink, and continued the celebration.

At 3:00 AM, Uncle Fred went upstairs to the bathroom. He noticed a light in the master bedroom; the door was partially open. He peeked inside. Lying on the bed with a smile on his face, his eyes staring upward, and his hands clutching a rosary was Hugh Ryan, dead.

38

THE DEATH CERTIFICATE handed to Bill by Dr. Cahill read "Heart Attack" under the caption entitled "Cause of Death." Bill looked at it hard, not knowing what was wrong. The doctor, noticing Bill's grimace, asked if there was a problem.

"I think so," said Bill, hesitating a few seconds to collect his thoughts and solidify some vague impressions. "My father didn't die of a heart attack. He was murdered—an organizational murder, if you like."

Dr. Cahill nodded knowingly, patted Bill on the head, and walked into the kitchen to console Margaret.

It was difficult for the Ryans, despite their traditional Irish view of life, to accept this tragic death; Hugh was only fifty years old. He still had young children and could have lasted for years if he had been treated with decency and respect. This was not a good wake; it was an angry one. Only Margaret saved it, her courage and grace sustaining weaker members of the family rather than them supporting her.

Bill was particularly agitated, calling McGlick's office regularly, identifying himself and asking to speak to the murderer. He even drove to headquarters, without his weapon, but was prevented from seeing McGlick by several officers stationed in the area because of his calls.

It took Uncle Fred nearly two days to calm the young man and bring him back to his senses. Bill had then fallen into a reflective mood; he sat by the hour, not as if in a trance, but in serious thought, aware of those around him but struggling with his own feelings and commitments.

On the morning of the funeral, Bill was able to smile again. He had resolved his inner conflicts and was at peace with himself. The family had gathered at the funeral home to say its final farewell before the church service. The distant relatives, then the cousins, then the immediate family knelt, said a prayer, touched the body, and then turned and left the room. Bill walked with his mother, the last to say that final good-bye.

Bill held his mother tightly as she bent over and kissed her husband gently on the forehead, saying, "I love you, Hugh." For the first time in three days, tears covered her cheeks in public. Bill would say the last farewell. He couldn't cry in public, though he cried uncontrollably in his heart. As he bent over and kissed his father for the first time in his adult life, he removed the family nightstick from its hiding place under his jacket, positioned it in the palm of his father's right hand, and then gently forced his father's rigid fingers around the stick. Then, slowly closing the lid of the coffin, he said, "I love you, Dad."

The family nightstick was to be buried forever.

1956   Raoul's prayers were answered. He was sentenced to life imprisonment, due in part to his cooperation in the Ryan matter. Mrs. Hector Rodriguez was awarded $50,000 by the Supreme Court, which ruled that the city's negligence was a contributing factor in her husband's suicide.

1957   Chief Inspector Terence McGlick was forced into retirement, after insulting the police commissioner during a meeting with the mayor at City Hall.

1958   Former Chief Inspector Yates was a hit-and-run victim on Staten Island near his home. He would be an invalid for life.

1959   Retired Police Captain Marvin Adler, living in Florida, was nearly lost at sea, having fallen off a fishing boat. Two days later, one Angelo Gallucci of Brooklyn was found DOA in a Miami swamp with two bullet holes in the back of his head.

1960   A retired police officer known as Silent Tony had his palatial Palm Beach home burglarized. The floor of the master bedroom had been ripped up, but the distraught man claimed that nothing was missing.

1961   Sergeant Rogers retired and moved to San Francisco.

1963   Retired Chief Inspector Terence McGlick was declared "totally insane," and was committed to an asylum.

1964   Uncle Fred was promoted to produce manager by the A&P. He became the original "We-oo" man.

1979   Margaret sold the big house in the Bronx, after raising all her children and seeing them through college. She moved in with one of her married daughters who owned a home in Upstate New York. Bill was now a captain in the NYC Police Department. Bill and Mary had five children and still lived in the Bronx.

1982   September 1

Bill was sitting in his office in the Forty-first Precinct station house. A large figure sat across the desk from him. "You have only two options, Bill," said the inspector, "either take the chief's offer and testify that Captain Russo is incompetent and get your promotion, or testify truthfully, and run for your life."

Later that afternoon, Bill testified that Russo was a good commander. As he left the courthouse with Mary, Bill held his thumb upward toward heaven, saying, "That one's for you, Dad." Mary smiled, squeezing his arm. "Are you going to retire now?" she asked. "No way," said Bill, prematurely gray at forty-three. "I still have one or two good fights left inside me."

1986   Bill's oldest son, Tom, is now twenty-one years old and a sophomore in college. He knows that the family nightstick was buried with his grandfather years earlier. He knows his father wants him to finish college and go into aviation. He also knows that he would love to be a cop, the first fifth-generation cop in the history of the NYC Police Department.

CPSIA information can be obtained
at www.ICGtesting.com
Printed in the USA
BVHW091601270722
643146BV00003B/560